AMAZING
BIOME
PROJECTS

YOU CAN BUILD
YOURSELF

Donna Latham

Illustrated by Farah Rizvi

To Lenore Marcotte, my BFF and fellow Temperate Zoner.
It's been a glorious journey!

Special thanks to Tom Pray, Pam Otto, Kathy O'Malley, and my husband Nick Longo for graciously sharing their experiences and time. With enthusiasm, energy, and wit, they are shining examples of Earth's Explorers who make a difference.

Nomad Press
A division of Nomad Communications
10 9 8 7 6 5 4 3 2 1
Copyright © 2009 by Nomad Press
All rights reserved.

This book was manufactured by Transcontinental Gagné,
Louiseville Québec, Canada
September 2009, Job #35928
ISBN: 978-1-9346703-9-2

Illustrations by Farah Rizvi

Questions regarding the ordering of this book should be addressed to
Independent Publishers Group
814 N. Franklin St.
Chicago, IL 60610
www.ipgbook.com

Nomad Press
2456 Christian St.
White River Junction, VT 05001

green press

INITIATIVE

Nomad Press is committed to preserving ancient forests and natural resources. We elected to print *Amazing Biome Projects You Can Build Yourself* on 4,315 lb. of Rolland Enviro100 Print instead of virgin fibres paper. This reduces an ecological footprint of:

Tree(s): 37
Solid waste: 1,057kg
Water: 100,004L
Suspended particles in the water: 6.7kg
Air emissions: 2,321kg
Natural gas: 151m3

It's the equivalent of:
Tree(s): 0.8 American football field(s)
Water: a shower of 4.6 day(s)
Air emissions: emissions of 0.5 car(s) per year

Nomad Press made this paper choice because our printer, Transcontinental, is a member of Green Press Initiative, a nonprofit program dedicated to supporting authors, publishers, and suppliers in their efforts to reduce their use of fiber obtained from endangered forests.

For more information, visit www.greenpressinitiative.org

FSC
Recycled
Supporting responsible
use of forest resources

Cert no. SW-COC-000952
www.fsc.org
© 1996 Forest Stewardship Council

Other titles from Nomad Press

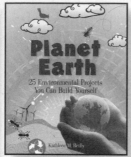
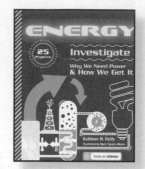

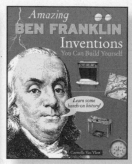

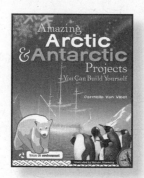

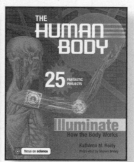

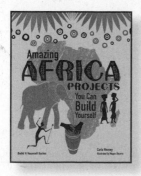

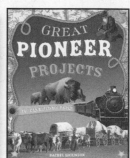

CONTENTS

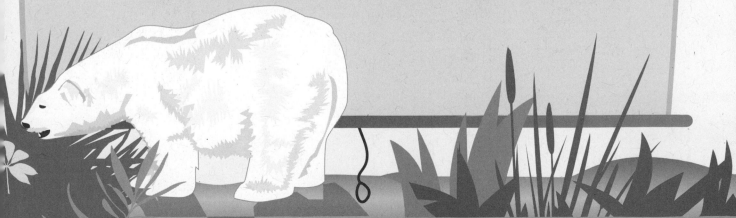

GREETINGS,
Eco Explorer!

Grab your backpack! You're about to embark on an exciting expedition to explore Earth's major **biomes**. A biome is a large natural area with a distinctive **climate** and **geology**, and specific water resources.

Each biome features its own **biodiversity**, a range of living things ideally suited for life there. For example, forests cover about a quarter of the planet. Yet different locations and climates mean you'll bound alongside snowshoe hares in one forest biome and leap along with red-eyed tree frogs in another.

Words to Know

biome: a large natural area with a distinctive climate, geology, set of water resources, and group of plants and animals that are adapted for life there.

climate: average weather patterns in an area over a period of many years.

geology: the rocks, minerals, and physical structure of an area.

biodiversity: the range of living things in an ecosystem.

1

Get ready for a wild and woolly adventure in extreme regions. You'll zip across continents, hover over volcanoes, and creep through brush. Along the way, you'll learn about environmental threats to biomes and what you can do to help.

First, you'll wander the planet's magnificent forests. Then you'll battle the blazing sun and scorching temperatures in sizzling desert areas. Later, you'll shiver in Earth's frigid, desolate regions. Many of these places are downright hostile to living things like you!

As you **circumnavigate** the globe, you'll learn about the **flora** and **fauna** in each biome. Plants and animals are perfectly built for survival on their home turf. Along your way, meet the world's precious endangered animals, and discover why they face **extinction**.

Extinction

You won't encounter a woolly mammoth or a mastodon traipsing through your neighborhood. These mega-mammals are extinct. When an animal or plant **species** becomes extinct, that means it's gone forever.

There are many causes of extinction. Natural occurrences, such as volcanic eruptions and climate change, can be factors. Animals may also become extinct when their homes or food sources are destroyed, or when people overhunt them. Sometimes, an **invasive species** disrupts their community.

How do invasive species enter an **ecosystem**? Consider the snakehead fish. These **predators**, dubbed "Frankenfish," are native to Asia. But people in the United States buy snakehead fish for their aquariums. As the snakeheads grow larger, they often devour

word exploration

The prefix **eco-** comes from the Greek word *oikos*, meaning house. Eco- refers to **environments** or **habitats**. For example, ecology is the study of the relationship between living things and their environment. Ecologists study ecology. What other words do you know that contain eco-?

their tank mates. Frustrated owners release them into ponds and lakes, where the snakeheads quickly make themselves at home. They disrupt the delicate balance of the local ecosystem. Snakeheads chomp insects, fish, reptiles, and birds. That leaves less food for other animals to eat and endangers them.

Scientists Classify At-Risk Plants and Animals

RARE Only a small number of the species is alive. Scientists are concerned about the future of the species.

THREATENED The species lives, but its numbers will likely continue to decline. It will probably become endangered.

ENDANGERED The species is in danger of extinction in the very near future.

EXTINCT IN THE WILD Some members of the species live, but only in protected captivity and not out in the wild.

EXTINCT The species has completely died out. It has disappeared from the planet.

Words to Know

circumnavigate: to travel completely around something.

flora: the plant life in an ecosystem.

fauna: the animal life in an ecosystem.

extinction: the death of an entire species so that it no longer exists.

species: a type of animal or plant.

invasive species: a non-native plant or animal species that enters a new ecosystem and harms it.

ecosystem: an interdependent community of living and nonliving things and their environment.

predator: an animal that hunts another animal for food.

environment: everything in nature, living and nonliving, including plants, animals, soil, rocks, and water.

habitat: a plant or animal's home, which supplies it with food, water, and shelter.

Earth's Explorers

What is Portuguese explorer Ferdinand Magellan's (1480-1521) claim to fame? He was the first person to circumnavigate the world. On September 20, 1519, he set sail from southern Spain with a fleet of five ships and 270 men.

Like many people of his time, Magellan badly misjudged the earth's size. He didn't realize the planet is enormous, with a **circumference** of 24,901 miles (40,074 kilometers). Magellan mistakenly believed he could sail across the vast Pacific Ocean in a speedy three days. That treacherous leg of his voyage actually lasted four grueling months!

As Magellan's journey around the world dragged on, his exhausted crew faced difficult conditions. There was disease and shrinking food supplies. An awful diet of rats, sawdust, and leather pieces ripped from the ships' sails kept crew members from starving to death. In 1522, three remaining ships and 115 men returned to Spain. Sadly, Magellan didn't survive the historic voyage.

One Earth, Many Biomes

The **biosphere** is the area of the earth and its **atmosphere** that is inhabited by animals and plants. Biomes are subsections, or smaller parts, of the biosphere. Within each biome live many ecosystems.

Visualize a skateboard. It's built of different connected parts that work together to keep you rolling along. What happens when a ball bearing flies off? The wheel pops off and the skateboard skids to a halt. When one part fails, the whole skateboard is affected.

An ecosystem works the same way: living and nonliving things depend on one another. Living things are plants and animals, while nonliving things include air, rocks, soil, the sun, and water. All parts of the ecosystem interact with their environment and among themselves. Teamwork keeps their complex, interdependent system balanced and working.

Earth's biomes are connected together, creating a vast web of life. As they sprawl across the globe, biomes blend. For example, tropical savannas mingle with deserts, and coniferous forests spill into the tundra. When natural or manmade disasters like volcanic eruptions or oil spills take place in one biome, they often have an effect upon other biomes as well.

Have you ever set up a line of dominoes? If you knock over one domino, it knocks down the second one. The second one knocks down the third one, and so on.

Whenever something happens in one biome, it launches a similar domino effect. The change sweeps through other biomes. How? Imagine a massive sandstorm as it whirls across Africa's Sahara Desert. A huge, hazy dust plume billows higher and higher into the sky. Winds blow the dust across the Atlantic Ocean. When the wandering cloud blots out the sun, it cools the ocean waters. This can cause a tropical storm to develop. Torrential rains and violent winds then clobber the Gulf Coast of Florida—all because of a sandstorm in Africa!

In this book, you'll read about climate, the factor that determines what living things inhabit a biome. You'll dig into soil, a critical component that controls the types of plants that grow there. And you'll encounter plants and animals and learn how they've **adapted** to the particular conditions of their biome.

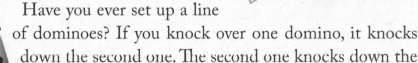

Words to Know

circumference: the distance around a circle.

biosphere: the area of the earth and its atmosphere inhabited by living things.

atmosphere: the mixture of gases that surround a planet.

adapt: changes a plant or animal makes to survive in new or different conditions.

terrestrial: related to land.

aquatic: related to water.

Biome Briefs: Ready Reference

As you explore each chapter in this book, be sure to return here to Biome Briefs, your ready reference chart. The "Where on Earth?" column lists the geographical locations of major biomes. The "Climate" column tells

LAND BIOME	WHERE ON EARTH?	CLIMATE	DESCRIPTION
Deciduous Forest	Canada, China, central and eastern Europe, Japan, Russia, eastern United States	full range of temperatures second-rainiest biome with 29-59 inches annual rainfall	four distinct seasons rich soil deciduous and broadleaf trees
Coniferous Forest	Asia, Canada, Europe, Russia, northern United States	cold and dry with a range of temperatures 35 inches annual rainfall	short summers and long, bitter winters poor soil coniferous trees including pines
Tropical Rainforest	Coastal Australia, Central and South America, Pacific Islands, Southeast Asia, West Africa	rainiest biome with at least 79 inches annual rainfall	year-round rainfall & warmth greatest biodiversity poor soil
Desert	Australia, Africa, Asia, Israel, Iran, Iraq, Mexico, southwest United States, western South America	driest biome, arid less than 10 inches annual rainfall	depending on location, can be hot or cold extreme changes in temperatures in hot deserts
Temperate Grassland	Australia, Canada, Europe, Asia, New Zealand, South America, United States	temperatures can vary greatly 20-35 inches annual rainfall	defined seasons mostly grasses with extremely few shrubs and trees
Tropical Savanna	Africa, Australia, India, South America	warm and dry with seasonal droughts 20-50 inches annual rainfall	two seasons—rainy and dry mostly grasses with scattered shrubs and trees
Tundra	primarily in the Northern Hemisphere: Alaska, Canada, Europe, Asia, coastal areas of Antarctica	coldest biome just 5-9 inches annual rainfall	two seasons—winter and summer layer of permafrost covers the ground
Mountain	on every continent and in every ocean	varies according to life zone	varies according to life zone

you what kind of weather conditions you should expect on your journey. After reading a quick description of each biome, you can learn about the environmental threats that each biome faces. Then find out how each biome's plants and animals have adapted to life in their special environments.

ENVIRONMENTAL THREATS	PLANT ADAPTATIONS	ANIMAL ADAPTATIONS
acid rain clearing for farmland and timber	trees and plants shed leaves for winter and go dormant	hibernation migration thick winter coats
acid rain clearcut logging fires	branches allow snow to slide off thick bark protects against fire waxy leaves seal in moisture dark green color captures sunlight	camouflage long legs migration webbed paws
overhunting deforestation for homes and mining habitat destruction	buttresses support huge trees leaves have drip tips so rain runs off waxy leaves protect against heat leaves capture sun	camouflage hanging out in the canopy where there's plenty to eat
cactus-collection climate change desertification ranching and overgrazing	pleated stems suck up & store water whiskery leaves prevent water loss	staying in the shade or in cooler burrows nocturnal activity extra-large ears store fat
farming overgrazing wildfires	grasses have narrow leaves to prevent water loss supple stems blow easily in the wind hardy roots enable regrowth after fires	animals build burrows camouflage to blend in with grassy backgrounds
desertification ranching and overgrazing wildfires	corky tree trunks stash water for dry periods grasses grow quickly after fires, since roots are protected underground	camouflage hoofed mammals have long legs to gallop away from predators and fires
air pollution climate change drilling and mining	grasses, lichens, mosses, and shrubs stay small plants hug the ground for warmth and to avoid wind	blubber insulates animals from cold camouflage to blend in with snow woolly fur keeps animals warm smaller ears hold in heat
habitat destruction mining	*Krummholz* and flagged trees grow in odd shapes perennials live more than two seasons	extra fur protects toe pads woolly fur with oily coating keeps animals warm extra large lungs take in more oxygen

Where on Earth?

Explore the world map to discover where Earth's major biomes are located. Notice how one biome rolls into another.

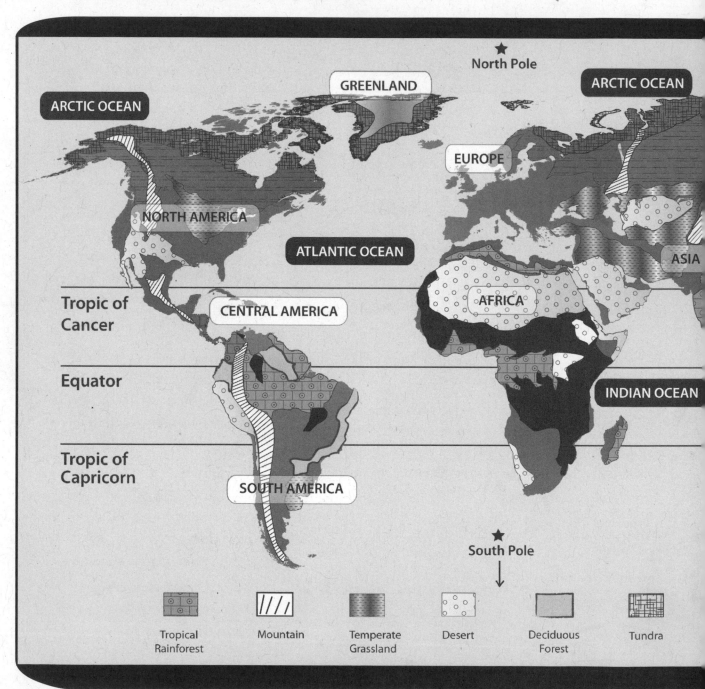

About the Projects

In this book you'll explore the earth's major **terrestrial** and **aquatic** biomes. You'll venture into the great outdoors to investigate your amazing home environment, as well as create indoor projects.

Don't forget that you're a crucial part of the earth's web of life. People affect every part of the world. Unfortunately, our impact isn't always beneficial. When you trek outside remember to treat your surroundings with respect. Take care to leave the area in the same condition you found it.

As you get down and dirty with the projects, notice that many of them use household and recyclable items. Reuse two-liter bottles, plastic deli tubs, and cereal boxes to make your own tornado in a bottle, to germinate seeds, and to decorate totem poles.

Flex your creative muscles and discover substitute materials for the projects. Don't have recyclable gloves for the blubber mitt project? Try plastic bags secured at your wrist with a rubber band. Can't locate a cardboard wrapping paper tube to create the rainstick activity? No worries! Try a paper towel tube instead. Or maybe one of your neighbors hoarded a length of hollow plastic tubing left over from a fix-it project. What kind of musical sound would that produce . . . ?

Of course safety comes first. Ask adults for help when handling kitchen chemicals, hammers, or any other supplies and equipment that might be dangerous. Science provides wonderful opportunities to investigate our wondrous world. So have fun!

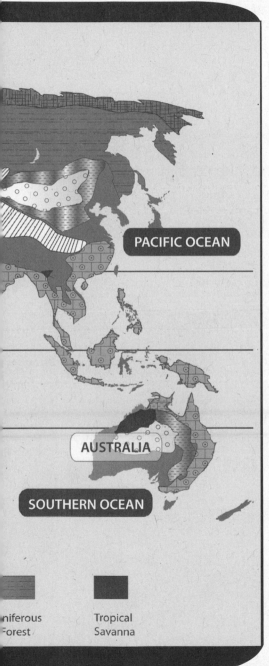

PACIFIC OCEAN

AUSTRALIA

SOUTHERN OCEAN

niferous
Forest

Tropical
Savanna

Chapter 1

HOME SWEET HOME

Earth is the only planet we know of with the ability to sustain life. Animals and plants inhabit nearly every nook and cranny of the global ecosystem. You're a vital part of a living planet. Turn back to the map on page 8, and locate your home turf, your region. In which biome do you live?

We enjoy a cozy partnership with the planet. Earth provides us with precious resources. In return, we must use these resources wisely and protect our planet.

What do living things require for survival? They rely on the sun's energy, light, and heat. They depend on water, food, and the atmosphere, which contains the necessary **elements** of oxygen, carbon dioxide, and nitrogen.

DID YOU KNOW?

We can't plop gargantuan Earth on a scale to weigh it, but scientists calculate its weight at 6.6 billion trillion tons. That's 21 zeroes!

It can be tricky to maintain a balanced partnership with our planet. Earth's growing population uses more and more of its resources. Many people treat our world with great care. But many others don't. Our behaviors and technologies can impact and cause great harm to the environment.

Scientists continue to study the environment and the ways humans affect the planet. Some scientists believe human activities are causing sweeping changes on Earth. Others believe the planet is experiencing part of a natural cycle. There are no easy answers or simple solutions. You can consider the theories, examine the available information, and form your own ideas.

Your Home Turf

Go outside and look around. Do you spot prickly pears, gently swaying palm trees, or patchy lichens? Do you hear waves lapping onshore or the buzz of bustling city streets? Which birds do you observe—honking geese flying in V formation, gobbling wild turkeys, or squabbling pelicans? What's scuttling over land—iguanas, Key Largo woodrats, squirrels and deer, or wadded clumps of paper that pollute the streets?

Notice how your area or neighborhood flows. Does one cornfield roll into another? Do streets with houses, apartment buildings, and shops connect to roads with parks and schools?

Words to Know

element: a basic substance, such as gold or oxygen, made of only one kind of atom.
atom: the smallest particle of all matter.

AMAZING BIOMES

Biomes are the earth's communities. If you could hover above the planet like a hummingbird, you'd notice that each biome blends into another. How many biomes does our bountiful planet boast? That's debatable. Some scientists believe it's five, while others root for 12. Still others think it's more accurate to divide Earth into hundreds of **ecoregions**.

One fact is certain: Biomes constantly change. From Earth's earliest history, biomes have undergone transformation. Natural events have always played a role. For example, floods have washed away coastal areas. Droughts have shriveled prairies and turned soil to dust.

Humans have changed things too. As people settle areas, they require shelter and food to survive. People have cleared forests to create space for homes and farmland. As populations boomed, they drained swamps and marshes to plant more crops, build businesses, and construct roads. They hunted animals to feed growing families and to provide furs to trade.

Today, people are increasingly aware of the delicate balance of life on Earth. Many are devoted to conserving our natural resources and preserving our biomes. As you read and explore, ponder the environmental threats that place our biomes and our planet at risk. Consider your own role in the world. Ask yourself how you can play a part to keep Earth thriving.

DID YOU KNOW?

You're probably aware that enamel, the hardest substance in the human body, covers and protects your teeth. Enamel is about 97 percent calcium. In contrast, iron coats beavers' rough, tough incisor teeth. Iron makes beavers' chiseling choppers orange in color and strong enough to gnaw through massive trees.

SAVE OUR PLANET!

Perfectly Adapted!

When you imagine a desert, you probably don't think of a furry polar bear. This burly beast couldn't survive such extreme heat. And the Arctic isn't where you'd expect to find an armor-plated armadillo. It's simply not built to endure frigid conditions.

Through **adaptation**, animals develop the right kind of physical features and behaviors to survive in their habitats, or homes. They've learned to live with the weather, build homes, steer clear of predators, and attract mates.

Aquatic animals such as beavers are adapted for life in water. When busy beavers build underwater lodges, they seal their eyes and noses shut with a special valve. They flap hefty webbed feet to swim. They are just right for water work.

Plants are also adapted for survival. Try catching a whiff of the endangered corpse lily, found in the rainforests of Sumatra. It smells exactly like rotten meat. While the putrid stench might knock us off our feet, it's perfect for attracting beetles and flies that distribute the corpse lily's pollen. A sweet deal for a smelly plant!

As you explore the earth's biomes, you'll discover many other amazing plant and animal adaptations.

word exploration

Armadillo is a Spanish word meaning "little armored one."

Words to Know

ecoregion: a large area, smaller than a biome, that has its own climate, geology, plants, and animals.

adaptation: the development of physical or behavioral changes to survive in an environment.

Make Your Own
PAPIER-MÂCHÉ GLOBE

Earth isn't just your home. It also provides the precious natural resources you need for survival. Our planet seems huge and invincible, yet it's surprisingly vulnerable, or open to harm. A globe is a 3-D model of the earth that includes its continents and oceans. This project will take several days or more to complete.

1 Cover your work area with newspaper. Blow up the balloon and tie it off with the string.

2 In the bucket or tub, mix 1 cup of flour with 2 cups of water. Stir it with the paint stick. Aim for a gooey consistency like a soft-boiled egg. You might need to add more water to make it just right.

3 Rip some newspaper into strips about 1 inch (2.5 centimeters) wide and 3 inches (7.5 centimeters) or so long. Dip each strip into the paste and run it between your finger and thumb to wring out the excess paste. Then wrap each strip around the balloon until you've completely layered the balloon. Smooth out the surface.

4 Wrap the balloon with three more layers of gluey strips. Then set the balloon aside, and allow it to dry for several days.

5 When the globe is dry, pop the balloon with the needle. Gently tug it with the string to remove it from the globe.

6 Spread newspapers over your work area again. Refer to the map or globe to locate continents and oceans. Sketch continent boundaries on your dried balloon. You might want to practice on a sheet of paper first. Paint the continents green and oceans blue. It's a good idea to paint the continents first, let them dry overnight, and then paint the oceans. That way, the colors won't ooze together.

7 Allow the globe to dry for at least 24 hours. When the globe is totally dry, use the marker to label continents and oceans. Select a special spot to display your globe.

Supplies

plenty of newspaper	long needle
balloon	flat map of the world or globe for reference
piece of string	
bucket or plastic tub	pencil
measuring cup	tempera paints
flour	paint brushes
water	black permanent marker
paint stick	

Make Your Own
RECYCLED PAPER

This is a two-part activity, and this first part is messy. After you create your own recycled paper, go outside to Investigate Your Home Turf in the activity on the next page.

1 Rip the paper into teeny pieces. Place about ½ cup of the paper into the blender. Pour about 2 cups of hot water over it. Repeat this process until the blender is halfway full. Cover the blender, and set it at a low speed. Mix the paper and water until it reaches a pulpy consistency. If the blender gets sluggish, then add a bit more water.

2 Carefully take your pulp outside with the rest of the supplies. Spread newspaper on a flat surface, and a towel or rag over it. Set it aside for a moment.

3 Pour the pulp into the pan or sheet. Slip the screen into the bottom of the pulpy liquid. Carefully press the screen to the bottom of the pan. Wiggle it back and forth until pulp coats it. Gently lift the screen from the pan or sheet, and allow the excess pulp to drip off.

4 Set the screen on top of the towel and newspaper from Step 2. Keep the screen's pulpy side up. Layer the second towel or rag and more newspaper on top of the screen, creating a "sandwich." Use the rolling pin to press on the "sandwich" from one end to another until you've wrung out all the water.

5 Spread out the third towel or rag in a warm, dry spot, and carefully place the "sandwich" on top of it. Allow it to dry for 24 hours. If you live in a humid place, it will probably require more time. When the paper is completely dry, peel the newspaper and towels from the paper. Use this homemade recycled paper in the activity on the next page.

Supplies

newspaper, old wrapping paper, or other scrap paper

measuring cups

blender

hot water

at least three large towels or absorbent rags

pan or cookie sheet with sides

an old piece of screen that will fit inside the pan or cookie sheet

rolling pin

Investigate
YOUR HOME TURF

Supplies

homemade paper from the
last activity
glue

1 Go outside and ramble around your
home, school, a park, or a natural area.
Drink in the sights and sounds of your
environment. Does the scenery include
mountains, ravines, prairies, or ponds?
What are the weather conditions? What
kinds of plant and animal life do you
observe?

2 Gather a few natural items as you
stroll. Perhaps you'll discover a pine
cone or acorn on the ground. Or maybe
you'll find a cool leaf or a feather, or a
pretty flower to press. If you live near
the ocean, scout around for a shell.
Please don't remove any animals from
their habitats, though.

3 Decorate the paper you made in
the last activity with the little treasures
you harvest from your trek but leave
some space in the
middle. Psssst!
Stash the
paper away
for now. Save
it for the last
activity
in this
book.

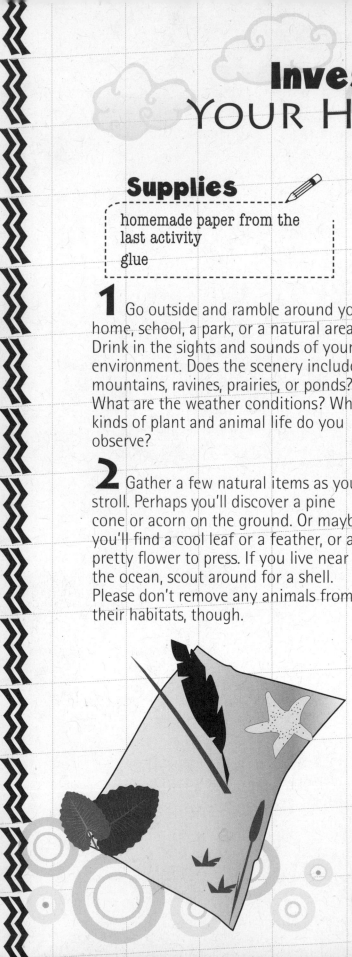

DID YOU KNOW?

This year alone, Americans will
use 85,000,000 tons (77,110,703
metric tons) of paper. In the
average American household,
people will toss 13,000 pieces of
paper into the garbage each year.

Chapter 2

DECIDUOUS
FORESTS

Trees, trees, and more trees! These woody wonders define the three different forest biomes you'll visit on your worldwide journey. First stop is the **temperate** deciduous forest. Seasonal changes characterize this biome. A long warm growing season is followed by a cold winter. Each year, **deciduous trees** shed their leaves as the weather gets colder. But today, the weather's a perfect 75 degrees Fahrenheit (24 degrees Celsius)!

This is one of the earth's most pleasant places, where humans have thrived for thousands of years. You'll find temperate deciduous forests in the eastern United States, Canada, China, Japan, Russia, and central and eastern Europe. These areas are all in the **Northern Hemisphere**. The soil is **fertile** in these forests, and the biodiversity is wide.

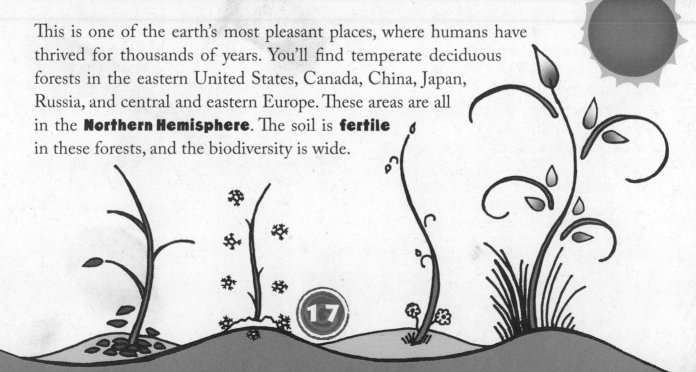

Food Chains and Food Webs

Every ecosystem contains **organisms** that interact with one another. One way they intermingle is through feeding patterns. Which animal feasts on which? **Food chains**, which illustrate feeding relationships, show you. Let's take a look at the food chain in the deciduous forest.

Plants are the foundations of the food chain. They are called producers, because they make their own food. They do this by capturing the sun's energy in a process called **photosynthesis**. Plants deliver the sun's energy to the animals and people who eat them.

Next in the chain are consumers—animals that can't make their own food. There are three different kinds of consumers in the deciduous forest. **Herbivores**, such as rabbits, beavers, and grasshoppers, munch only plants. Tasty stems, seeds, grasses, flowers, and fruit provide them with the nutrition they need.

Words to Know

temperate: not extreme in terms of climate or weather.

deciduous trees: trees that shed their leaves each year.

Northern Hemisphere: the half of the planet north of the equator.

equator: the imaginary line around the planet halfway between the North and South Poles.

fertile: rich in nutrients and good for growing plants.

organism: something living, such as a plant or animal.

food chain: a series of plants and animals connected by their feeding relationships, with each new link in the food chain depending on the link below as a source of food.

photosynthesis: the process through which plants create food, using light as a source of energy.

herbivore: an animal that eats only plants.

decomposers: bacteria, fungi, and worms that break down wastes and dead plants and animals.

nutrients: substances that organisms need to live and grow.

omnivore: an animal that eats both plants and animals.

carnivore: an animal that eats only other animals.

food web: interrelated food chains.

competition: the struggle between living things for food, water, sunlight, and other resources.

The Poop on Decomposers

Let's not forget the lowly **decomposers**. They tackle a gross job, but somebody's gotta do it. Decomposers even dine on animal waste . . . yep, poop. Creepy bacteria, funky fungi, slimy slugs, and wriggly worms also digest and break down dead wood, leaves, plants, insects, and animals. Then they pass **nutrients** from these decaying carcasses back into the soil. Plants grow by absorbing these nutrients, and the circle of life continues.

Omnivores, such as skunks and wild boars, eat both plants and animals. **Carnivores** eat only the meat of other animals. These hunters include cougars, wolves, and owls.

Food chains illustrate a straight line of what-munches-what. But **food webs** are more complex. For instance, a rainforest food chain begins with a leaf. A beetle eats the leaf. A red-eyed tree frog then swallows the beetle. And a bat devours the frog. That's a food chain. But snakes like to eats frogs too. Bats and snakes are competing for the same food source. The food chain has now grown into a food web.

In any ecosystem, different species not only compete for food but also for sunlight, water, and even mates. **Competition** is the struggle for resources between different species or among members of the same species.

Dig It! Here's the Dirt on Soil

The soil in the deciduous forest biome is dark brown and fertile. What's soil like in your neck of the woods? Depending on where you live or which biome you visit, you'll discover different types. Soil might contain clay, sand, or silt. These components of soil determine its texture, or how gritty and clumpy it feels. Why is texture important? In sandy soils, water and nutrients drain away rapidly. Dense soils are more fertile, but they can become waterlogged.

DID YOU KNOW

Covered with copper and metallic green shells, dung beetles are attractive decomposers. Their habits? Uh, not so much. Dung beetles nestle into fresh animal **dung** to chow down, make their homes, and lay their eggs. The **larvae** are worm-like baby beetles. When they hatch, their first meal is ready, all around them.

Soil covers the planet's land surface and is necessary for life. Soil might look, well, dirty, but it's actually full of nutrients, living organisms, and decaying organisms. Soil is **porous**, meaning that it's filled with teeny holes or spaces. When rainfall pelts soil it flows through all those holes, dissolving nutrients along the way. Thirsty tree and plant roots then slurp the nutrients up.

Which living organisms of the deciduous forest dig soil? Moles do. With their itty-bitty eyes and webbed paws shaped like shovels, they tunnel through the ground and **aerate** the soil. Their tunnels let air circulate. Moles like to dig for their favorite snack, juicy earthworms.

Burrowing badgers also work the soil, like little striped farmers. Their work creates larger tunnels for rainwater to enter the soil and give thirsty plants a drink.

If you could burrow into soil like a mole on a mission, you'd encounter four layers, or horizons. Plants and animals inhabit the ground level, or **topsoil**. Fertile topsoil is a blend of silt, sand, clay, and **organic matter**. In this layer, seeds sprout and plants take root.

Have you ever turned over a clump of topsoil and noticed it's cool to the touch? That's because leaf litter, grasses, and other plants protect topsoil from getting too dry. When plants die, insects such as ants, spiders, centipedes, and termites chomp them up into teeny bits.

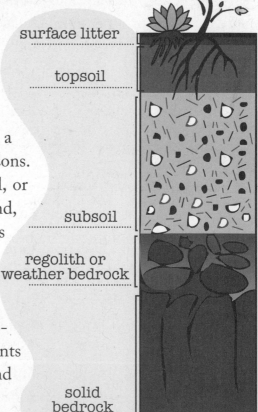

surface litter

topsoil

subsoil

regolith or weather bedrock

solid bedrock

DID YOU KNOW?

Before gulping a worm, a mole stretches it like a rubber band between clenched paws. Why? To squish yucky grit from the its gut.

Decomposers also break down wastes and dead plants and animals and recycle them into **humus**. Not to be confused with hummus, the delicious dip you slather on pita bread, chocolate-brown-colored humus is organic matter. Rich in nutrients from de-composed plants and animals, humus allows new plants to grow.

The second layer is **subsoil**. Minerals and humus mingle together here. You'll also find thirsty roots meandering through sticky clay and weathered rocks as they work to locate a water source.

The third layer is **regolith**, or weathered bedrock. Weathered means it's been ex-posed and worn away by weather's activi-ties. In this case it would have been a long time ago, before all that soil was on top. This deep layer contains no organic matter. Plant roots can't break through this rocky, mineral-filled horizon.

The bottom level is **solid bedrock**. This unweathered rock hasn't been exposed to the elements. How could it become weathered? If an earthquake blasts it to ground level or water erosion wears away upper levels.

Words to Know

dung: solid animal waste.

larvae: the worm-shaped form of a young insect (like a caterpillar) before it becomes an adult.

porous: full of many little holes so water passes through.

aerate: to create channels that allow air to flow through.

topsoil: the top layer of soil.

organic matter: decaying plants and animals.

humus: decaying organic matter made from dead plant and animal material.

subsoil: layer beneath topsoil.

regolith: layer of loose rock, also called weathered bedrock.

solid bedrock: layer of solid, unweathered rock.

Try This

Go outside, and with a hand shovel or a large spoon, carefully turn over a clump of soil. Eyeball the sample. Do you see any insects or worms? Streaks of sand or bits of gravel? Now, rub the soil between your fingers. What's the texture—grainy, mushy, rocky? When you're finished, gently place the sample back, and pat it in place.

Four Distinct Seasons ... With Trees to Match

A temperate climate experiences a full range of temperatures. Although temperatures may dip to -20 degrees Fahrenheit (-29 degrees Celsius) and peak at close to 100 degrees Fahrenheit (38 degrees Celsius), the average is 50 degrees Fahrenheit (10 degrees Celsius).

Yearly rainfall ranges from 29 to 59 inches (74 to 150 centimeters). During frost-free months, plant life flourishes.

Deciduous forests are nestled between the northern polar regions and the southern tropics around the equator. Because of the earth's rotation and the sun's slant, temperate deciduous forests enjoy four distinct seasons, each with characteristic weather. Both frosty Arctic air and warm tropical air whoosh across the zone at different times of the year and impact the climate.

In temperate climates, snowy winters and hot summers are typically the same length. Yet, even with this dependable pattern, people in temperate zones expect major fluctuations. Temperate Zoners often say, "Don't like the weather? Just wait a minute and it will change."

In the deciduous forest biome, trees change with the seasons. In winter, trees are **dormant**. During the warm, wet spring, buds bloom with flashy flowers.

Water Worlds

A marsh is a type of freshwater wetland commonly found in the deciduous forest biome. Located in low-lying, waterlogged areas, marshes border lakes, ponds, and streams. Plants and animals thrive in marshes. For example, reeds and cattails grow in and around them. Reeds are tall, stalky grasses, while cattails are plants with thick stems, long shoots, and bristly seed heads. Herons and cranes, two types of large birds, also inhabit marshes. Demonstrating adaptation to their environment, they use their long legs to slosh through waters and search for food.

Broadleaf trees, which bear flowers and fruits, are designed to catch the sun's rays during the summer months. In the autumn, these trees shed their leaves.

Forest Strata

The deciduous forest has many levels. It's like a high-rise apartment building packed with different residents. The top level earns bragging rights for having the best sunlight. The farther down you roam, the dimmer the light becomes.

The forest is divided into five main layers, or **strata**. On top is the **canopy**. It teems with the leafy branches of tall, mature trees that capture as much sunlight as possible. Broadleaf trees, including maples, oaks, and chestnut trees, extend up to 100 feet (30 meters) tall. They shove aside smaller competitors for sunlight and create a cover of shade across the forest like a giant patio umbrella. Great horned owls perch atop trees for a birds-eye view of unsuspecting **prey** on the forest floor. Further down, in some of the lower "apartments," bears doze in cozy nooks.

The second layer is the **understory**, made up of saplings, or young trees. Here, blue jays screech and squirrels somersault from limb to limb like acrobats.

Words to Know

dormant: when plants are not actively growing during the winter.

strata: layers of the forest.

canopy: an umbrella of trees over the forest.

prey: animals hunted by other animals.

understory: the second layer of the forest, made up of saplings.

Threats to Deciduous Forests

Deciduous forests face many threats. Some of them are natural, such as climate change, disease, forest fires, and insects. And some of the threats come from humans. For thousands of years, people have chopped forests for timber or burned them to create farmland.

Some scientists believe acid rain is the greatest threat to the deciduous forest. When pollutants from vehicles and factories merge with water droplets in the air, the result is acid rain. Acid rain is snow or rain with deposits of acid. This kind of precipitation injures leaves and weakens trees. It slows their growth and causes them to produce fewer seeds.

How can you help preserve deciduous forests? You can conserve paper, which is made from trees. For instance, don't throw away paper when you make a mistake. Instead, use both sides of a sheet. And don't forget to recycle paper and newspapers.

The third layer is the shrub layer, which contains shrubs and bushes. It's a key rest stop for plant-loving animals, including squirrels and chipmunks, which munch on crunchy greens and fruits.

Lower down, the herb layer features herbs, short plants, and berries. These provide tasty treats for famished raccoons, mice, and voles. Flowers also bloom here, attracting bees and hummingbirds looking for nectar.

The fifth layer is the forest floor, or carpet. Dark and chilly, the floor is covered with leaf litter. Decomposers such as mushrooms and termites break down decaying leaves and plants and contribute to the biome's fertile soil.

Words to Know

chlorophyll: a pigment that makes plants green, used in photosynthesis to capture light energy.

migrate: to move from one environment to another when seasons change.

hibernate: to sleep through the winter.

Deciduous trees are transformers, which means they can change in order to endure bitter winters. During the fall, food production shuts down for the season like an ice cream stand closing up. **Chlorophyll**, a pigment that gives leaves their vivid green hues, breaks down. Trees display their "fall colors" until the leaves flutter down to join their buddies on the leaf pile.

In winter's chill, trees become dormant. Growth screeches to a halt, and vegetation appears to snooze away the frigid months. Fortunately, trees plan ahead for the winter. During the summer months they turn extra food into starch and stockpile it for wintry days. Then when spring fever descends on the biome, trees crank back into food-production mode.

word exploration

Deciduous comes from the Latin word *decidere*, which means "to fall off." No wonder autumn is also called FALL.

Adapted to Seasonal Change

During autumn, many birds flee the cold and **migrate** to balmier biomes to the south. But not all deciduous forest animals get out of town. Some **hibernate** for the winter, while others hang around and make a few changes to their routines. Without lush greenery to conceal them, animals must adapt to hide from predators. The least weasel, for example, sprouts a snow-white coat for a winter disguise.

Meanwhile, squirrels pack on an extra 20 percent of their body weight to help them survive the harsh winter. Have you ever stumbled upon a mound of acorns hidden beneath a bush? You probably encountered a secret squirrel stash. Squirrels stow munchies in a cache, or food-hiding place, and dip into the hoard throughout the winter.

Science in Action! Meet Pam Otto, Naturalist

In winter, the snow-covered ground is frozen, and icy winds howl through bare trees. Ecosystems are dead, right? Not on your life! Meet Pam Otto, naturalist and outdoor education specialist at the St. Charles Park District in Illinois. Pam's crazy about nature. Her eyes sparkle with enthusiasm as she chats about **subnivian** life beneath the snow.

BIOMES: Pam, what happens underground when snow covers the forest floor? The ground looks totally lifeless.

PAM OTTO: When the first snow falls, the ground is still warm, about 32 degrees Fahrenheit. It's not exactly balmy for us, but what an opportunity for life! Snow melts and creates a little layer called the subnivian zone. Subnivian means "beneath snow." It's an open space between the snow and the ground. It's only about an inch, but insects take advantage of that protective layer, away from the cold and snow. It's also where meadow voles live.

BIOMES: What's a meadow vole?

DID YOU KNOW

The effects of acid rain can be far-reaching. For example, coal-power plants in the southern and midwestern United States produce pollution that doesn't just impact those regions. Instead, pollution moves with the wind to the northeastern United States, where it falls as acid rain. For this reason, we have the Clean Air Act, which are the laws that help us keep our air clean.

PAM OTTO: I call it a little baked potato! It's a small, stocky rodent, similar to a mouse, but with a pudgy body. Underground, the voles munch buried seeds and plant debris. They chomp insects, too. Voles are important to the food chain. Hungry minks and weasels gobble voles and mice. Shrews prey on voles, too. Shrews have carnivorous

Words to Know

subnivian: the ground area below a layer of snow and above soil.
forage: to wander from place to place in search of food.

26

DID YOU KNOW

Scientists nicknamed owls "flying tigers" because these predators are so highly adapted for hunting. Owls boast the toughest set of feet in the bird world. When an owl pounces on prey such as a vole, its powerful talons pierce the skull. Owls carry prey back to their roosts, where they swallow it in one gulp.

teeth—large and pointy. Larger predators, such as coyotes, foxes, hawks, and owls prey on voles, too. With its powerful sense of hearing, coyotes listen to life underground. The coyote stops, tilts its head, and listens. When the coyote's ready, it pounces like a cat.

word exploration

Wile E. is a play on the word wily, which means "crafty and sly."

BIOMES: Speaking of coyotes, Pam, why do so many roam residential areas these days?

PAM OTTO: Coyotes are super-adaptors. Remember the cartoon character Wile E. Coyote? Wile E. is an apt name. Coyotes move to an area and take advantage of all it has to offer. Their range expands in winter, when they have to wander farther to **forage** for food. They don't mind scouting areas where people live. If people intentionally or unintentionally leave food outside, well, coyotes don't have to fight the food to grab it. And it doesn't bite them back!

BIOMES: If we take a closer look at the ground, will we spot evidence of subnivian drama beneath our feet?

PAM OTTO: When snow melts in the springtime, look for winding tunnels. They're highly used pathways.

DID YOU KNOW

Hummingbirds are airplanes for mites, which are tiny relatives of spiders and ticks. As the hummingbird flits from flower to flower, a teeny eight-legged mite zips into its nostril to hitch a ride.

Make Your Own
FOOD CHAIN FLIPBOOK

Create your own animated mini-movie to illustrate a deciduous forest food chain in action.

1 First, use the scratch paper and pencil to plan the animation. Cast plant and animal actors from the temperate deciduous forest biome. Jot down a plant to launch the chain. A fern, a clump of grass, a bit of moss, for example. Add a plant-loving animal to chomp the green stuff. Perhaps a grasshopper? Now, think of an omnivore to pursue the herbivore, and so on. Which mighty predator tops the chain— and ends the action? The longer the chain the more fun you'll have.

2 Count the number of sheets in your pad of paper, and plan an equal number of drawings. Make sure there are at least 25 sheets. This will zip the action along for a spectacular show! Plan a sequence of events to illustrate links in the food chain.

Supplies

scratch paper

pencil

small pad of thick paper; at least 25 sheets, unlined

markers

3 Sketch the sequence on scratch paper to practice. Remember to use both sides of the paper! Each illustration should be a little bit different from the one before it.

4 Then, draw the sequence on the pad. Put one image on each sheet, and keep it as near the edge of the page as you can.

5 Continue drawing until the action concludes. If you want to get really involved you can color your illustrations with the markers. Just make sure to keep the colors consistent from one page to the next.

6 You're ready to roll! Hold the flipbook in one hand. With the thumb of your other hand, grip the book, and ruffle the pages from the front to the back.

28

Chapter 3

CONIFEROUS
FORESTS

You've discovered that one biome rolls into another. Let's roll northward into the gorgeous coniferous forest. You're now standing in the largest terrestrial biome on Earth.

Words to Know

coniferous trees: cone-bearing trees, often with needles for leaves. These trees do not lose their leaves each year.

boreal forest: another name for the coniferous forest biome.

taiga: another name for the coniferous forest biome.

evergreen: a tree that keeps its leaves or needles throughout the year.

Coniferous trees, which don't shed their leaves each year, define this biome, which is also called the **boreal forest** or **taiga**. At its southern end, the coniferous forest mingles with **evergreens** in deciduous forests. In the northern end, the coniferous forest merges with the treeless Arctic tundra.

Water Worlds

Bogs are bodies of water that form over decomposing plants and **peat**, which is waterlogged decomposed material. Bog waters contain large amounts of acid, and the soil below them is low in nutrients. Some plants, including shrubs, mosses, wild rice, and cranberries, grow in bogs. Other plants, such as the sundew and pitcher plant, perform extreme adaptations for survival. These carnivorous plants trap and gobble insects to take in nutrients.

An Unbroken Band

Scientists describe the coniferous forest as an unbroken band of trees. Located in the Northern Hemisphere, it encircles parts of Asia, Canada, Europe, Russia, and the United States. It's like a green wreath, 50 million acres (20 million hectares) in size.

There are two types of coniferous forest—closed canopy and open canopy. In closed-canopy forests, trees grow in close, tight huddles. They shade the mossy carpet. In open-canopy forests, trees are scattered and amply spaced. Instead of velvety mosses, patchy gray-green **lichens** sprawl over the forest floor.

The coniferous forest is a close kin of the deciduous forest. How do the two biomes differ? While deciduous forests enjoy four distinct seasons, coniferous forest climates experience speedy summers and lengthy winters. The growing season is a scant three to four months.

word exploration

Conifer comes from the Latin word *conus,* which means "cone," and *ferre,* "to bear."

Words to Know

peat: waterlogged, decomposed organic matter.
lichen: a patchy plant that is a combination of fungi and algae.

Winters linger for six freezing months, with temperatures plunging down to as low as -40 degrees Fahrenheit (-40 degrees Celsius). Fleeting summers only get as high as 70 degrees Fahrenheit (21 degrees Celsius). Chilly temperatures result in slow decomposition, so soil tends to be rocky and spongy or waterlogged instead of packed with the nutrients found in humus.

Adapted for Looong, Dry Winters

While deciduous trees shed their leaves, conifers bear cones. Cones hold seeds and scaly needles. Many conifers, also called evergreens, remain gloriously green all year round. Cedar, cypress, fir, larch, pine, and spruce trees abound in the coniferous forest. Hardy deciduous trees such as aspen, poplar, and birch squeeze in here and there.

How do conifers adapt to survive prolonged, brutal winters? Their deep, dark green coloring helps evergreens capture as much of the sun's light as possible. A waxy coating on their needles protects them from drying out in wintry winds.

word exploration

Boreal is a Greek word that means "north." *Taiga* is a Russian word meaning "swampy pine forest." Swampy areas such as marshes and bogs cut through coniferous forests. Lakes do, too.

Evergreens must take advantage of every minute of the brief growing season, so they cling to their needles all year. They don't have time to shed their needles in the fall and then sprout them again in the spring. Instead, when springtime warmth finally blusters in and more water becomes available, evergreens are ready to crank up photosynthesis.

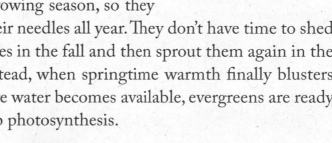

Try This

Go outside to investigate! First, gently pluck a needle from an evergreen tree and run your fingers over the surface. Do you feel its waxy armor? Try to pinch out a bit of sap, the sugary liquid that flows through plants. Any success? Pine needles contain just a smidge of sap, which keeps it from freezing in the winter. Now, compare the branches of a deciduous and a coniferous tree. Which is more flexible, or easier to bend? You should discover that the coniferous branch is more pliable.

Evergreens are pointed and narrow at the top and wide and full at the bottom. Thanks to this cone shape, snow swooshes off an evergreen's bendable branches like a snowboard off a slope. This adaptation means snow can't accumulate and crack branches under its weighty load.

Weather Flash—Lightning!

In summer, lightning frequently flashes above the coniferous forest. It ignites wildfires, which are often fueled by dried needles. Thick bark helps protect trees against scorching flames, but destruction can be widespread.

Living in the Coniferous Forest

There is not a lot of biodiversity in the coniferous forest. Fewer species exist here than in deciduous environments. During the short summer months, vegetation provides plenty to munch on. Woodpeckers, ravens, and hungry herbivores including elk, muskrats, and snowshoe hares pluck juicy treats from blackberry bushes. Meanwhile, predators such as endangered Siberian Tigers, grizzly bears, rare lynx, and wandering wolves feast on plentiful prey. Peregrine falcons (also endangered) swoop from their rocky ledges to snatch dinner off the forest floor.

When winter blasts in, some animals migrate. For example, the grosbeak, a finch with an extra-large, seed-snapping beak, flies south. Other animals adapt. The snowshoe hare trades its brown summer coat for a white one that blends in with snow. With this **camouflage**, it remains one hop ahead of the lynx. To maneuver in snow, both animals scramble on long legs. Webbed paws act as built-in snowshoes.

Words to Know

camouflage: the colors or patterns that allow a plant or animal to blend in with its environment.

pelt: animal skin.

overhunting: when an animal is hunted in great numbers, so much that their population falls to low levels. This can cause extinction.

clearcut logging: a process in which all or almost all the trees in an area are chopped down.

Try This

Find a pine cone and allow it to dry out in the sun for a day. Then, plop the pine cone into a paper bag. Shake the bag thoroughly. Open it up, and presto! You'll discover the seeds at the bottom of the bag. Plant them in honor of the coniferous forest biome.

Threats to Coniferous Forests

Many of the species that inhabit this biome are furry mammals. Their striking **pelts** and tasty meat have been desirable for centuries. **Overhunting** has put many of these animal populations in peril. For example, today the Siberian tiger is a rare species because people hunted them to excess. Scientists believe fewer than 400 Siberian tigers remain in the wild. Musk deer and caribou have also been overhunted and now face reduced populations.

Clearcut logging also threatens the coniferous forest. When people clear land for homes, farms, or industry, they sometimes remove nearly ever tree. Clearcut logging wipes out habitats and creates soil erosion, which is the wearing away of soil by water and weather. When soil erodes, it loses its top layers, which are full of nutrients. Along with those layers, soil loses its ability to grow plants.

Drawn by its natural beauty, many photographers, artists, hikers, and campers visit the coniferous forest biome. Unfortunately, visitors are sometimes careless with campfires, which can lead to dangerous forest fires.

The best way to build a campfire is to use enclosed campfire pits provided by forest preserves, or to create a circle of rocks around a pit area. The smaller the fire, the easier it is to contain. When you're done, drown the flames with a bucket of water. Stir the fire with a shovel, douse all glowing embers, and drown the fire a second time. Always use extreme care when building a campfire, and never do it without an adult.

JUST FOR LAUGHS

Q: How did you find the weather in the coniferous forest?

A: I just went outside, and there it was!

DID YOU KNOW?

The world's oldest living organism just happens to be a conifer. Ancient Methuselah, a bristlecone pine, grows in California's White Mountains. The location is kept a secret because scientists are afraid someone might try to snip a souvenir from the tree. How mature is mighty Methuselah? Nearly 5,000 years old! That's the age of Egypt's ancient pyramids.

Make Your Own
PINE CONE BIRDFEEDER

Go outside and scout around for a plump pine cone. Then use the cone's seed case to make a birdfeeder, and observe the birds that swoop in for a crunchy snack.

Supplies

- plate
- birdseed
- pine cone
- butter knife
- peanut butter or sunflower butter
- 3 feet of string
- journal
- pencils and markers

1 Place the plate on a flat surface or tabletop and sprinkle birdseed over it.

2 Use the butter knife to spread peanut butter over the pine cone. Fill in the little nooks and crannies.

3 Roll the peanut-buttery cone over the birdseed until it's completely covered with seeds.

4 Select a prime location for bird watching out your window. Then tic one end of the string to the top of your pine cone. Tie the other end to a sturdy tree branch.

5 Observe the birds that visit your feeder. Jot down descriptions in your journal, and create sketches. Use online or print references to identify the feathered friends that flit to your feeder for a snack.

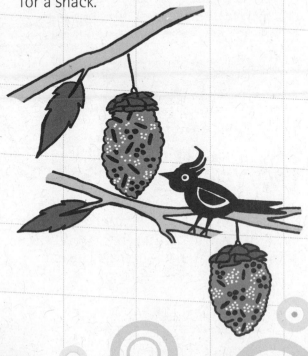

DID YOU KNOW

Pine nuts are edible conifer seeds that are packed with protein. They're favorites in dishes around the world, including Korean jat juk, Greek baklava, Italian pesto, and Middle Eastern kibbeh.

Make Your Own
EXPERIMENT WITH ACID RAIN

Acid rain is a major environmental threat to forest biomes. In coniferous forests, acid rain injures tree needles and impairs their ability to survive frigid winter temperatures. Here you'll use vinegar, which is an acid, to conduct an experiment about the way acid rain affects plant growth.

Supplies

scissors
cardboard egg carton
permanent marker
potting soil
vinegar
water

4 jars
fast-growing seeds, such as green beans, lima beans, or radishes
journal and pencil

1 Use the scissors to carefully cut away four "compartments" from the egg carton. You can recycle the rest of the carton. With the marker, number the compartments from 1 to 4. Label each as follows:

1. W only   3. 1W–1V

2. 5W–1V   4. V only.

This stands for:
1. Water only
2. Five parts water to one part vinegar (for example, 5 cups water mixed with 1 cup vinegar)
3. One part water to one part vinegar (for example, 2 cups water mixed with 2 cups vinegar)
4. Vinegar only

2 Fill each compartment with potting soil, and plant the seeds in each. Prepare the four jars with the water and vinegar combinations to correspond with the four egg carton compartments.

3 Copy the chart into your journal. What will happen to the seeds when you water them with each of the liquids or liquid combinations in the "Watered With" column? Jot your **hypothesis** in the appropriate column.

Words to Know

hypothesis: a possible idea or explanation about something that you test in an experiment.

4 Water the seeds each day with the appropriate liquids. After one week, note the progress of each compartment of seeds. Describe your findings in the "One Week" column. Add a small sketch to accompany your description. Repeat after two weeks, and update the chart.

5 Compare and contrast the plants yielded by the seeds. What effects do different levels of acid cause? What conclusions can you draw about the effects of acid rain on plants?

WATERED WITH	HYPOTHESIS	ONE WEEK	TWO WEEKS
1. Water only			
2. Five parts water to one part vinegar			
3. One part water to one part vinegar			
4. Vinegar only			

DID YOU KNOW

Amber, the beautiful golden-orange material used to create jewelry, is made of fossilized conifer resin. Some chunks of amber contain spiders, insects, and plants preserved inside.

Make Your Own
PAST, PRESENT, AND FUTURE TOTEM POLE

Native Americans have inhabited coniferous forests for centuries. In the Pacific Northwest, they used towering cedar tree trunks to carve magnificent totem poles. Totem poles told important stories about heroes or chiefs. You can create a Past, Present, and Future totem pole to tell tales about yourself. At the bottom, show something memorable that happened in your past. In the center, share a special moment from your life right now. At the top, include a dream for your future.

1 Reseal the opened tops of the boxes with glue. Then cut and glue construction paper to completely cover each of the three boxes. Use the scissors to trim paper as needed to cover the front, back, sides, tops, and bottoms of the boxes.

2 With the paints, illustrate your Past, Present, and Future tales on the manila paper. Glue the completed illustrations onto the front of each cereal box.

3 Use the found objects to decorate the illustrations. Do you have some odds and ends stashed in a junk drawer? This is a good time to reuse them!

4 Stack the boxes in the correct order as you construct the totem pole. The Past goes on the bottom, Present in the middle, and Future on top. Use glue to attach the three boxes together, bottom to top.

5 Make wings out of the manila paper for the Future illustration. Decorate the wings. Make a fold about an inch wide on the straight edge of each wing. Glue one wing to each side of the box.

6 Scout out a cozy spot to display your totem pole. Use it to tell your stories to your family and friends, and let your dreams take flight!

Supplies

- glue
- three empty cereal or cookie boxes of identical size
- construction paper
- scissors
- tempera paints and brushes
- manila paper
- treasures and found objects such as beads and buttons, stickers, toy parts, game pieces, fabric remnants, feathers

Chapter 4

TROPICAL RAINFORESTS

Let's journey south now to the world's rainiest biome, the tropical rainforest. Although rainforests cover only 7 percent of the earth's land surface, half of the planet's animal and plant species make their homes here.

Tropical rainforests are located near the equator, between the **Tropic of Cancer** and the **Tropic of Capricorn**. Go back to the map on page 8 to see where these are. You'll find tropical rainforests in Australia, Central and South America, the Pacific Islands, Southeast Asia, and West Africa. Tropical rainforests experience little fluctuation in temperature. Frost never develops in this moist, hot biome, and plants never become dormant. Average rainfall is 80–160 inches (203–406 centimeters), while the average temperature is 80 degrees Fahrenheit (27 degrees Celsius).

Words to Know

Tropic of Cancer: a line of latitude north of the equator, marking the northernmost point at which the sun can appear directly overhead at noon.

Tropic of Capricorn: a line of latitude south of the equator, marking the southernmost point at which the sun can appear directly overhead at noon.

DID YOU KNOW

The equator is an imaginary line around the widest surface of the earth, at its center. The Tropic of Cancer and the Tropic of Capricorn are two imaginary lines of **latitude**, or horizontal lines on a map. The Tropic of Cancer is located about 23.5 degrees north of the equator, while the Tropic of Capricorn is about 23.5 **degrees** south.

Words to Know

latitude: imaginary lines around the earth parallel to the equator.

degree: unit of measure of latitude. One degree of latitude equals 1/360 of a circle. The North Pole is 90 degrees north latitude, while the South Pole is 90 degrees south latitude.

buttresses: thick, aboveground roots that support tall trees.

torrential: flowing intensely in large quantities.

Living in Levels

Like its deciduous cousin, the tropical rainforest is multi-leveled with different flora and fauna at each layer. The top level is the emergent layer, where mushroom-shaped treetops burst out of the forest. Colossal broadleaf trees tower 250 feet (76 meters) in the air.

These green giants support their own weight as well as the load of all the critters that live in them. How do they pull this off in the rainforest's shallow, soggy soil? They have thick, aboveground roots called **buttresses**. These massive, woody feet fan out around the base of trees as natural supports.

The emergent layer is home to bats, butterflies, harpy eagles, howler monkeys, and snakes. What's the benefit of living up there? That's where the most sunlight is.

DID YOU KNOW

The harpy eagle can reach speeds of 50 miles (80 kilometers) per hour when it dives on prey, such as iguanas and monkeys.

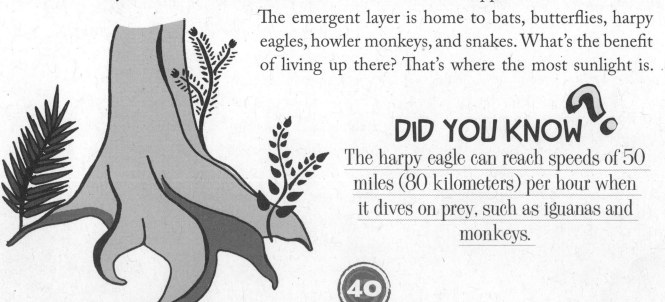

On the flip side, though, it's pummeled with fierce winds and **torrential** rains. The top level also endures incredible heat.

In this hot, moist environment, bacteria and fungi grow quickly, so decomposition is speedy. It's important that healthy plants shed water quickly so they won't decay. Leaves are adapted with pointy drip tips that let rainwater run off quickly.

The next level down is the canopy, which is shaped like an open umbrella. Here, broadleaf trees stretch toward the sun, some peaking at 90 feet (27 meters). Most rainforest animals hang out in this bustling and colorful level, where sunlight—and noise—is abundant. Colorful toucan birds munch on tasty leaves, fruits, and nuts. Sluggish sloths hang upside-down by hooking tree limbs with curved claws. Hummingbirds, including those who migrated from deciduous forests for the winter months, slip needle-nose bills into flowers to sip sweet nectar.

Let's move down. Flying, gliding, leaping, and swinging are the best ways to travel here. Snag a sturdy vine, and swoop through the understory. Smaller trees and shrubs compete for space in this cooler, damp layer, where sunlight is limited.

Emergent Layer

Canopy Layer

Understory Layer

Forest floor

What Big Eyes You Have!

With its fluorescent green body, sky blue sides, orange feet, and bulgy red eyes, the three-inch, red-eyed tree frog is one of the Amazon rainforest's most recognizable creatures. Mini suction cups on its tiny feet are ideal for clinging to leaves in the canopy. The frog's peepers provide a type of camouflage called startle coloration. Here's how it works. By shutting its green eyelids, the little frog blends in with multi-colored leaves. When a snake slithers by, or a bird dives down, the frog's eyes suddenly spring open. The befuddled predator encounters a surprising set of googly crimson eyes. It hesitates for an instant—just enough time for the frog to make a speedy getaway into the leafy understory.

Plants grow gigantic leaves here, an adaptation that allows them to capture as much of the sun's energy as possible. Patchy lichens, ferns, and delicate orchids grow in this level. There are also insects, such as spiders, walking sticks, beetles, bees, and army ants. They provide tasty morsels for birds, lizards, snakes, and monkeys.

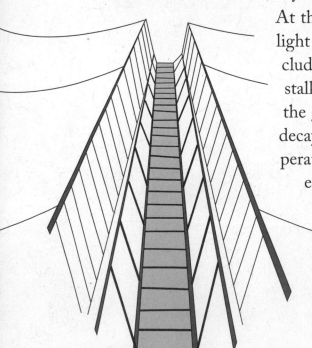

At the bottom level sprawls the forest floor. Little sunlight penetrates down here. Carnivorous predators, including agile jaguars and bone-crushing anacondas, stalk this dark level. Seeds, fruits, and branches fall to the ground, where herbivores devour them before they decay in the tropical heat. Unlike the rich soil of temperate deciduous forests, rainforest soil is low in nutrients. Why? Because pounding rains flush them away.

DID YOU KNOW?

Lianas are so thick and strong that people in the rainforest use them to build bridges.

Words to Know

liana: a woody vine that wraps itself around the trunks and branches of trees in an effort to reach the sunlight.

greenhouse gas: a gas that traps heat in the earth's atmosphere and contributes to the greenhouse effect and global warming.

Lianas, which are lanky, woody vines, hang throughout the rainforest. Lianas begin life as seeds scattered on the forest floor. As lianas grow, they drape themselves around trees and begin climbing high to soak in the sun's rays.

Threats to Rainforests

Scientists have nicknamed rainforests "the lungs of the planet." This is because the abundant plant life in the rainforest provides 20 percent of the world's oxygen.

It also cleans the air of carbon dioxide, a major **greenhouse gas**. How? Through the process of photosynthesis, plants use energy from sunlight, water from soil, and carbon dioxide from air to make their own food. Through photosynthesis, plants release oxygen—which people and animals need to breathe and live.

Gases such as carbon dioxide, methane, and water vapors permit the sun's rays to enter the earth's atmosphere. Yet, they trap the rays and produce heat. Like a greenhouse where plants grow, temperatures rise. They become hotter than outside air.

Greenhouse Gas

Try This

Did you know that you can raise tropical rainforest plants right inside your own home? Exotic houseplants such as African violets, Christmas cactus, prayer plants, and zebra plants are rainforest exports. They're adapted to the dim light of the forest floor, so they can tolerate low light in homes.

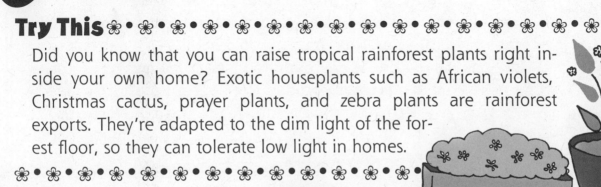

This process is called the **greenhouse effect**. We rely on the greenhouse effect to keep the earth warm enough to sustain life. However, when it gets too warm it can lead to climate change, which causes trouble for living things.

Earth's lungs are shrinking—fast. **Deforestation**, which is occurring at an alarming rate, threatens this biome. People clear land for mining, farming, and to build homes. As they do, they destroy habitats for thousands of precious species, including those that live in no other place on the planet. In fact, some scientists believe about 35 rainforest species become extinct each day as deforestation increases and human populations grow.

Words to Know

greenhouse effect: when gases such as carbon dioxide, methane, and water vapor permit sunlight to pass through but also trap solar radiation, causing the warming of the earth's surface.

deforestation: the process through which forests are cleared to use land for other purposes.

archaeologist: someone who studies ancient cultures by looking at what they left behind.

prehensile: able to grasp things.

Earth's Explorers

From 300 BCE to 900 CE, the Maya were one of the most powerful groups in Mexico and Central America. They built sophisticated cities with temples, statues, and pyramids, some as tall as 200 feet (61 meters). While priests lived in the cities, most people lived on farms. The Maya thrived in the heat and humidity of the rainforest. They developed a system of writing, devised calendars, and tracked the movement of the sun, moon, planets, and stars.

Suddenly, after more than 1,000 years, the Maya deserted their cities and farms. **Archaeologists** are investigating this mystery to discover why. One theory is that the Maya depleted their natural resources. Perhaps farmers eroded the soil in an effort to feed a growing population. When the soil wore out and maize, or corn, couldn't grow anymore, people moved in search of new farmland.

More Amazing Animal Adaptations

Meet the okapi, nicknamed the "forest giraffe." This rare animal is native to the Ituri Forest of Central Africa. With striped forelegs and hindquarters, it resembles a zebra. Yet, the okapi's long, **prehensile** tongue—adapted for grasping and yanking tasty leaves—provides a clue that it's related to the giraffe. Why doesn't the okapi have a giraffe's long neck and stilt-like legs? Because it has to dodge dangling lianas and chunky buttresses to forage for food. Lanky limbs and a stretchy neck would just get in the way!

DID YOU KNOW?

Many canopy animals never descend down to the forest floor. They stay high in the canopy their whole lives.

Speaking of tongues, don't forget Australia's echidna. This small spine-covered mammal forages across the forest floor, thrusting its snuffling snout into termite nests or anthills. Then it shoves a spiky tongue, coated with sticky saliva, inside. Nutritious insects get trapped on the gooey coating. The echidna reels in its tongue and smooshes the bugs into a pulp in its toothless mouth.

It's no surprise this egg-laying mammal has few predators. What happens when an enemy threatens the echidna? The super-speedy digger uses razor-sharp claws to tunnel out a hiding place, or else it curls up into a bristly ball that predators don't want to tussle with.

Water Worlds

Rivers are freshwater bodies that constantly move in one direction. They meander across land to reach another large area of water, typically the sea. South America's Amazon River, which flows through the rainforest into the Atlantic Ocean, is the world's longest river. The Amazon River is over 4,000 miles (6,400 kilometers) long.

One of the residents of its murky waters is the red-bellied piranha. Groups of piranhas team together to ambush large prey, including caimans and anacondas. They can strip prey to the bone in minutes.

Plant Your Own
HUMMINGBIRD GARDEN

Hummingbirds don't have a sense of smell. Instead, they respond to color, especially large groups of flowers in reds, pinks, and oranges. Let's plant a colorful garden and invite the world's smallest bird to visit!

With their teeny needle-nose bills, hummingbirds prefer trumpet-shaped flowers with slim, long necks. They especially love flowers oozing with nectar, their top food source. Do some research before you plant your garden. Find out which species of hummingbirds live in your area. Learn about the kinds of flowers that attract hummingbirds. Investigate which flowers will thrive in your location and won't be invasive species.

Supplies

flowers and shrubs suitable for your region	**FLOWER CHOICES**	**SHRUB CHOICES**
	bee balm	agastache
paper and pencil	bleeding heart	azalea
gardening gloves	bougainvillea	butterfly bush
shovel	coral bells	gooseberry
compost or store-bought humus	coral honeysuckle	lilac
	fuchsia	red-flowing currant
garden hose	hollyhock	Rose of Sharon
broken tree branches	impatiens	thimbleberry
	Indian paintbrush	
bucket	petunia	journal
old rag	red columbine	
birdbath	trumpet vine	

1 Locate a space for your garden, and choose flowers and shrubs suitable for your region. Use the paper and pencil to draw a plan for your garden. Divide the flowerbed into sections, and label where you will plant each item. Read the planting directions, so you'll know how much space to leave between each plant.

2 Put on the gardening gloves and use the shovel to dig holes in the soil. While you're at it, take a close look at the soil. Is there enough humus to help the plants grow? If there's not, you may have to add a bit of compost or some humus. Can you find bits of sand, clay, or gravel? How about wriggly worms and roly-poly bugs?

3 Following your plan, place each plant in the soil, and refill the hole. Pat the soil back into place.

4 Thoroughly water the garden daily with the garden hose. If you're lucky, a hummingbird might flit into the mist for a quick spritz! Hummingbirds enjoy misty sprays.

5 Stick the broken branches into the garden here and there to make perches for the hummingbirds. Find a safe perch nearby, such as a tree limb, away from prowling predators. Ask an adult to help you punch a small hole into the bucket. Tear off a small bit of the rag to stop up the hole. Then pour a small amount of water into the bucket, and hang it from the perch.

DID YOU KNOW?

When Spanish explorers encountered vibrant hummingbirds in the New World, they called them joyas volardores, or "flying jewels." It's an ideal description for the shimmery birds, which can flap their wings an average of 50 times per second!

6 Fill the birdbath with fresh water and place it beneath the bucket. Now, you have a dripping shower, where hummingbirds can hover to grab quick splatters. Provide fresh water daily. You might discover that hummingbirds prefer to splash in moist leaves, so keep your eyes peeled when you water your garden!

7 Observe the hummingbirds that visit your garden. In your journal, add sketches and notes to those that you made for your Pine Cone Birdfeeder.

Make Your Own
RAINFOREST
CRUNCH 'N' MUNCH

Use ingredients that come from rainforests to make this sweet and crispy no-cook snack. This recipe makes 22 quarter-cup servings.

1 Use clean hands to handle supplies and ingredients. Measure and pour the cereal, banana chips, pineapple, and nuts into the mixing bowl. Gently stir the mixture with the wooden spoon.

Supplies

measuring cups	½ cup cashews
mixing bowl	wooden spoon
1 cup rice cereal	¼ cup semi-sweet chocolate bits
1 cup corn cereal	
1 cup dried banana chips	¼ cup shredded coconut
1 cup dried pineapple	½ teaspoon ground cinnamon
½ cup Brazil nuts	airtight container

2 Sprinkle the chocolate bits, shredded coconut, and cinnamon over the top.

3 Serve with a spoon. Store the remaining mixture in a tightly sealed container for up to three days.

DID YOU KNOW

The abundant plant life of the rainforest doesn't just feed animals. It feeds people too. Bananas, Brazil nuts, coconuts, mango, papaya, and star fruit are all yummy rainforest foods. Is there a rainforest treat in your fridge or pantry?

DID YOU KNOW

Coconut, an important food in the tropics, is the fruit of the coco palm, considered one of the world's most useful trees. People use the coco palm's leaves to make thatched roofs, umbrellas, baskets, and fans. They carve coconut shells into beautiful bowls, cups, and ladles, as well as buttons for shirts and sweaters.

Chapter 5

DESERTS

You were drenched by torrential rains in Earth's wettest biome. Now, let's dry off in its most **arid** biome, the desert. In some deserts, blisteringly hot days transform into shivery nights, and parched landscapes explode into vibrant life when infrequent rainstorms sweep in.

About 20 percent of the planet's surface is comprised of deserts. You'll find them in many countries, including Australia, India, Israel, Iran, Iraq, and Mexico. They're also located in Africa and in the southwestern United States.

Extremely low levels of rainfall characterize the desert, where daily temperatures can career from a scorching 110 degrees Fahrenheit (37 degrees Celsius) during the day to a frigid 30 degrees Fahrenheit (-1 degree Celsius) at night. Why do temperatures nose-dive so drastically? Desert air is extremely dry. Because the air contains scant moisture, it's not able to cling to much heat. When the sun sets, temperatures plummet.

Desert Adaptations

In the extreme environment of the desert, survival is tricky. Soil is **coarse**, rocky, and salty. Plants encounter frequent **droughts**. The bristly Saguaro cactus has adapted to these harsh conditions by developing stems that are pleated like accordions. When rain makes a rare appearance, the pleats puff up. They suck the water in, stash it away, and tap into the supply during droughts. The Saguaro also has a waxy coating on its skin, which seals in moisture and cuts down on **transpiration**.

Meanwhile, Joshua trees use spiky, hairy leaves to protect themselves from the fierce sun and wind. These "trees" are actually members of the lily family, and can grow as high as 40 feet (12 meters). You can only find them in the Mojave Desert of Arizona, California, Nevada, and Utah.

In South Australia, the crimson Sturt's desert pea survives by using a vertical taproot. Rather than spreading out in shallow soil like a fibrous root, a taproot plunges straight down, seeking out water from deep in the ground.

DID YOU KNOW

What's the hottest temperature ever recorded? The Sahara Desert scored that honor when the thermometer soared to 136 degrees Fahrenheit (58 degrees Celsius) in 1922.

DID YOU KNOW

Native Americans used the Joshua tree's sturdy leaves to weave baskets and shoes.

Adapted for the Desert

How do animals survive in the dry, challenging environment of the desert? Most avoid the sun's heat by hanging out in shady areas around rocks and under shrubs, such as the creosote bush. Many animals are **nocturnal**, which means they scout around for food only at night. During the hot days, they hide out in cool **burrows** in the sand.

Ships of the Desert

Most desert animals are small, but there is one big animal that is built for survival in scorching heat. The camel! It's probably the most famous desert animal of all. And no wonder. Dubbed "ships of the desert," these hardy pack animals are adapted for trekking over sand. Their humps weigh up to 80 pounds (36 kilograms) and act as storage tanks for fat to use when food grows scarce. They also have three sets of eyelids. The top set is thin and transparent. The camel snaps it shut during fierce sandstorms. Long, curly eyelashes also help bat away blowing sand.

JUST FOR LAUGHS

Q: What do you get when you cross a cactus with a pig?

A: A porky pine!

Words to Know

arid: very dry, receiving little rain.
coarse: composed of large particles.
drought: long, dry spell without rain.
transpiration: the evaporation of water from plants, usually through tiny pores in their leaves called stomata.
nocturnal: describes an animal that is active at night instead of during the day.
burrows: underground holes and tunnels where animals live.
marsupial: a mammal that has a pouch where its young develop.

Most desert mammals are small. The big guys haven't adapted for life in this harsh biome. They're too bulky to duck into burrows to escape the sweltering sun, and they're not built for water storage.

Let's take a look at some of the ways desert animals have adapted to their environment. For example, what does the bilby, a **marsupial** from Australia, the jackrabbit of the American Southwest, and the fennec fox of Africa have in common? These pint-sized creatures all have jumbo ears! Big ears radiate heat, allowing it to escape from the animals' bodies so they can keep cool. The fennec fox also sports thick fur on its feet to protect it against the broiling hot sands of the desert.

Meanwhile, the leopard gecko (found in Iran, Iraq, and Pakistan) relies on its super-thick skin to keep from shriveling up like a prune in the dry desert. This insect eater uses its plump tail to store fat when food is scarce. But that's not all it does. When a ravenous predator, such as a fox or snake, grabs the gecko's tail, part of it comes off! This momentarily baffles the predator, giving the gecko an opportunity to scurry off. Losing a tail portion doesn't hurt the gecko, and later, the lost segment grows back.

And there's the vulturine guinea fowl, a native of Ethiopia. This electric-blue, red-eyed bird scored its name because its bare head looks like a vulture. It can endure long periods without water. How? By digging out and eating moist bulbs and seeds.

DID YOU KNOW

Like other members of the cuckoo family of birds, roadrunners have two toes that face forward and two that point backward. Perfect for dashing over sand to catch prey!

The roadrunner gets water from its food as well. You'll find roadrunners in the Chihuahuan, Mojave, Sonoran, and southern Great Basin Deserts, which are all located in North America. These speedy birds, members of the cuckoo family,

Water Worlds

A pond is a still, small body of water created by rainfall. In the arid desert, temporary ponds spring up during heavy rainfall, only to later dry up and vanish. Before ponds disappear, though, plants and animals take full advantage of them. Consider the Australian water-holding frog. It's adapted to stash water in its bladder and can live for nearly seven years on the supply. The frog burrows deep into the ground during droughts. It sheds a few layers of skin and uses them to cocoon itself. When a temporary pond develops, the water-holding frog devours its cocoon and travels to the surface of the water to breed.

can zoom at 15 miles (24 kilometers) per hour. They eat scorpions, lizards, and even deadly rattlesnakes. In fact, their long, slim bills are specially built to hold snakes far from the roadrunner's body. Why? So angry snakes can't strike them.

Threats to Deserts

Because of human activity and climate change, the desert is the earth's quickest growing biome. You know that what happens in one biome can impact another. **Desertification**, which turns fertile land into dry land, occurs in other biomes. This creates more deserts. Desertification can happen when people clear land for crops. By doing so, they also remove vegetation that protects soil from **erosion**.

Ranching also threatens other biomes and can turn them into deserts. Some people allow plant-munching animals to **overgraze**, which means all the plants are gobbled up. What's more, grazing animals' hooves pummel fragile soil and cause it to wear away.

DID YOU KNOW

The Atacama Desert of Chile and Peru is the world's driest place. How dry is it? Not even cacti grow there! The parched Atacama usually receives only one inch of rain each year.

Cactus-collection threatens the desert. Visitors to the biome, thrilled by beautiful and exotic cacti, yank them out of the sandy soil and sneak them home. It's against the law, and it often results in dead plants and dwindling species. What can you do to help? Purchase cacti at gardening and retail stores. Never take a cactus—or any plant—from its environment.

Words to Know

desertification: the transformation of non-desert into desert, usually due to lack of water, deforestation, and/or overgrazing.
erosion: the gradual wearing away of rock or soil by water and wind.
overgraze: when animals eat plants at a rate faster than the plants can grow back or be replaced by new plants.

Science in Action! Meet Kathy O'Malley

Kathy O'Malley is a senior research technologist at the Mayo Clinic in Rochester, Minnesota. Kathy went to extremes when she left temperate Minnesota and journeyed to the cold desert of the South Pole to study **altitude sickness**.

After flying 24 hours to Christchurch, New Zealand, where they were fitted with 75 insulating pounds of clothing, including goggles, Kathy's team flew another six hours to McMurdo Station in Antarctica. Finally, they travelled three additional hours to the South Pole.

The South Pole is 9,300 feet (2,835 meters) above sea level. Combined with the intense cold, the earth's spin creates extreme conditions that would occur at even higher **altitudes**.

DID YOU KNOW

Out on The Ice, you'll find monuments that honor some of Earth's Explorers, including Admiral Richard E. Byrd and Ernest Shackleton, who braved extreme conditions to journey to the planet's most inhospitable place.

BIOMES: Tell us about the purpose of your journey to Antarctica.

KATHY O'MALLEY: We studied about 240 volunteers to assess their reactions to high altitudes. McMurdo is at sea level, and we first conducted tests there. Then everyone took a plane to the South Pole, which is at a high altitude. We repeated the tests to see how people responded to changes in altitude. We collected **data** and later took it back to the Mayo Clinic to **analyze** it.

BIOMES: What happens to the human body at high altitudes?

Words to Know

altitude sickness: a medical condition that occurs in high altitudes. It is caused by low oxygen levels in the blood and tissues of the body. Its symptoms include fatigue, nausea, and dizziness.

altitude: height above sea level.

The Ice: the nickname for Antarctica.

data: information from tests or experiments.

analyze: to study and examine.

pulmonary edema: a medical condition in which the lungs fill with fluids and swell, making breathing difficult.

frostbite: a medical condition in which skin and other tissues of the body are damaged by being frozen or partially frozen.

KATHY O'MALLEY: There is less oxygen to breathe at high altitudes. People respond differently to the altitude sickness that results. It can even cause high-altitude **pulmonary edema**, which is like heart failure. I felt loopy, dizzy, light-headed, and sick to my stomach.

BIOMES: Just how cold was the cold desert?

KATHY O'MALLEY: Well, I'm from Minnesota, and I thought I was used to low temperatures! But out on The Ice, which is the nickname for Antarctica, it's really different. It's not the damp cold you feel to the bone. Instead, it's completely dry. You take your glove off to snap a photo and you wonder, "Why isn't my finger moving down? Oh, it's frozen stiff!" We always worked with a buddy so the partner could let us know if our faces were turning white. That would indicate that **frostbite**, a very dangerous condition, had set in.

BIOMES: What was the most memorable part of your experience?

KATHY O'MALLEY: The researchers all create a family environment—you eat together, exercise together, work together. It was lots of fun, and I made friends from all over the world, really unique people. It was truly a heart-warming experience in a frigid environment. One I'll never forget!

DID YOU KNOW

How cold can a desert get? One unforgettably frigid July day in 1983, the temperature plunged to a bone-rattling -129 degrees Fahrenheit (-89 degrees Celsius) in Vostok, Antarctica.

A Cold Desert?!

Isn't that an oxymoron? An oxymoron is a figure of speech that combines contradictory words, such as jumbo shrimp and serious fun. Cold desert sounds like an oxymoron because most people associate deserts with heat. But deserts aren't only about camels and tumbleweeds. Antarctica is the planet's coldest, driest, most blustery place. You wouldn't expect it to be a desert. But it is. It's a cold desert swathed in a permanent ice sheet that reaches a depth of 15,669 feet (4,776 meters). Antarctica receives nearly the same amount of moisture each year as the Sahara Desert!

Paint Your Own
PICTOGRAPHS

Write in pictures! A pictograph is a symbol used to represent a word or an idea. For example, the symbol of a lightning bolt stands for the word lightning. To tell tales, ancient people created pictographs on rock surfaces. Modern people have discovered pictographs all over the world, including the deserts of the American Southwest.

Have you ever used paint to leave your handprint? If you have, then you're not alone. One of the most common pictographs is the human handprint, a time-honored symbol that boasts, "I was here!" Through art, ancient people also honored the sun, moon, and stars. They celebrated successful hunts and even depicted extinct animals. How did ancient people mix pigments? They combined animal fat with berries, blood, charcoal, clay, and minerals such as chalk. Create your own chalk pigments to paint rock pictographs.

Supplies

several unusual rocks	measuring spoons
newspapers	water
2 large Ziploc bags	craft or Popsicle stick
chalk in a variety of colors	white glue
rubber mallet	corn husks, twigs, feathers
plastic deli containers or other plastic tubs	

1 Go outside and scout around for several interesting rocks of various sizes. Wide, flat rocks work well, but bumpy or grooved rocks are great too. Set them aside as you make your own paint.

2 Spread the newspaper over your work area. Then slip one of the Ziploc bags inside the other. Place one piece of chalk in the inside bag, and firmly seal both bags. Use the rubber mallet to carefully smash the chalk until it becomes fine powder. Try to hammer out any clumps.

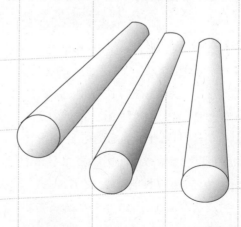

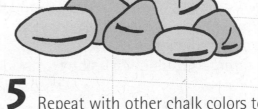

3 Pour the pulverized chalk into a deli container or plastic tub. Add 1 teaspoon of water. Use the craft or Popsicle stick to blend the powder and water until it's smooth.

4 Now add 1 tablespoon of white glue to the mixture. With the stick, blend the mixture. Slowly add water to achieve a smooth consistency. You will most likely need 2 or 3 tablespoons of water.

5 Repeat with other chalk colors to create a few different paints to work with. Use your creativity to blend new colors.

6 Use the corn husks, twigs, feathers, and your fingertips—all methods ancient people used—to paint pictographs on the rocks. You can research ancient pictographs for inspiration. Or you can devise your own symbols for people, animals, events, and activities that are important in your life.

DID YOU KNOW

Along with ancient pictographs showing birds, dogs, horses, lizards, and other animals are drawings of what may be extinct species. For example, cave art shows what scientists believe may be the mastodon, an extinct member of the elephant family, and the quagga, an extinct member of the zebra family.

Make Your Own
RAINSTICK

Rainsticks probably originated in Chile in South America. Here, people of the Atacama Desert may have been the first to fashion them from dried cactus stalks, thorns, pebbles, and wood. Desert dwellers performed music with the rainsticks to ask the gods to send precious rainfall during droughts.

Supplies

- cardboard wrapping paper or postal tube
- marker
- cardboard
- scissors
- glue
- masking tape
- aluminum foil
- rice
- lentils or dried beans
- popcorn kernels
- measuring cup
- funnel
- tempera paints
- paint brushes

~ Rain Stick ~

1 A long tube makes the best rain sounds, so use a wrapping paper or postal tube. Trace the end of the tube onto the flat cardboard piece. Repeat, so that you have two cardboard circles. Cut out the circles. These are the end plugs for your rainstick. Use the glue to attach one end plug. Reinforce it with the masking tape. If your tube already includes plastic or metal end plugs, then reinforce one end with masking tape, and set the other plug aside for step 5.

2 Measure a sheet of foil so that it's twice as long as your tube. Then, firmly roll the foil into a long, spiraling coil about ½ inch (1 centimeter) thick. Press the coiled foil into your tube. The coil is the rainstick's sound filter.

3 Pour a combo of rice, lentils or beans, and popcorn kernels into the measuring cup until you have about ½ cup. Slip the funnel into the open end of the tube, and pour the mixture inside. These will produce your rain sound.

4 Conduct a sound test. Use your palm to plug the open end and let the beans run from one end of the tube to the other. Is it music to your ears? You might want to add a bit more of the dried products—but don't make the rainstick too heavy, or it will be cumbersome to play.

5 With the glue and masking tape attach the second end plug. Then use the paint and brushes to decorate the rainstick with desert plants and critters. Don't stop there! Compose a rainstick rhythm and perform it.

Make Your Own
DESERTARIUM

Have you ever planted a terrarium, or a miniature garden, in a jar? Now, give your green thumb some exercise by building a desertarium, or a miniature desert!

1 Slip on the gardening gloves, and line the bottom of the container with a ½-inch (1-centimeter) layer of crushed charcoal. Charcoal soaks up odors and keeps the soil from becoming stinky. Cover the charcoal with a 1-inch (2.5-centimeter) layer of gravel or pebbles.

2 Now, combine two parts potting soil, one part sand, and one part compost. Spread at least 2 inches (5 centimeters) of this soil mixture over the gravel or pebbles. You'll probably notice the soil is a bit moist from the compost. Make sure it's only damp and not wet when you add the plants. When conditions are too wet, fungus can grow.

3 Plan an artistic landscape for your plants. With the garden shovel and your hands, form mounds and valleys in the soil.

4 Now add the plants. Handle cacti with care so the prickles don't pop through your gloves! Position the plants artistically in the mounds and valleys. Decorate the desert landscape with your pictograph rocks.

Supplies

- gardening gloves
- wide glass container, large fishbowl, or aquarium
- crushed charcoal from a gardening store
- gravel or pebbles
- potting soil
- sand
- compost
- garden hand shovel
- plants such as aloe vera, cacti, and jade
- pictograph rocks (from Paint Your Own Pictographs)

5 Place the desertarium in a sunny location. Cacti and succulents are relatively slow-growing plants. You won't need to closely tend them, but check from time to time to make sure they're thriving. Always leave your desertarium uncovered. That way, moisture will evaporate and conditions will remain dry as a bone.

Chapter 6

Temperate GRASSLANDS

Let's take a stroll through Earth's grasslands. This biome covers approximately 20 percent of the planet and can be found on every continent except Antarctica. Grasslands are usually found in the middle areas of continents, sandwiched between deserts and forests. Like forests, grasslands can be either temperate or tropical, depending on their location. Let's investigate temperate grasslands first.

Grasslands are treeless, wide-open spaces found north of the Tropic of Cancer and south of the Tropic of Capricorn. Depending where on Earth they're located, grasslands are referred to by many different names.

Earth's Explorers

Explorers Meriwether Lewis and William Clark were the first Americans to travel overland to the Pacific Coast and back. From 1803 to 1806, they described and illustrated hundreds of species that had never been scientifically recorded. They also shipped wildlife specimens home to President Thomas Jefferson, who was intrigued by science and nature. At that time, about 5 billion prairie dogs populated the Great Plains! Lewis and Clark, who called the critters "barking squirrels," even shipped a live one to President Jefferson.

Words to Know

prairie: term for temperate grassland, primarily used in Canada, but also in the United States.

plains: term for temperate grassland, primarily used in the United States, but also in Canada.

pampas: term for temperate grassland in South America, especially Argentina.

Eurasia: the land mass of Europe and Asia.

steppe: term for temperate grassland in Russia and the Ukraine.

veldt: term for temperate grassland in South Africa.

savanna: term for tropical grassland.

They sprawl over Canada's **prairies** and across the United States' **plains**. They stretch through South America's **pampas**, over **Eurasia's steppes**, and across South Africa's **veldts**.

Temperate grasslands can experience a wide variety of temperatures. Depending on the season, the thermometer might dip to -40 degree Fahrenheit (-40 degrees Celsius) or climb to 100 degrees Fahrenheit (38 degrees Celsius). The winters can be cold and dry and the springs wet with rain. The soil here is rich, but biodiversity is lower than in the tropical **savannas** you'll visit next.

DID YOU KNOW

It's hard to build houses without trees, but the pioneers who settled the prairie found a solution. They constructed their homes out of dirt and grass! These sod huts were called soddies. First pioneers tunneled a hole into a hill. Then they made a roof with grasses and branches chopped from scattered trees. Finally, with chunks of sod cut from the vast prairie, they covered the roof and erected walls. Pioneers shared their soddies with grassland fauna, including field mice and rattlesnakes. What happened if soddies leaked in rainstorms? Industrious pioneers patched them with mud, clay, and more sod.

Amber Waves of Grain

Unlike forests, where trees are dominant, grasslands are full of grasses, such as barley, buffalo grass, coneflowers, oats, pampas grass, and wheat. When the wind blows over the plains of the American Midwest, for example, you'll see waves of grain fluttering over huge, flat expanses of land. The soil here is bursting with nutrients, and is ideal for growing corn, oats, and wheat. These crops are used to produce breads and cereals for the entire country. No wonder this part of the country has been called "The Nation's Breadbasket."

There's plenty to eat here for animals, too. Large grazing herbivores and many insect species live in grass-lands. For example, you can find bison, elk, pronghorn, wild burrows, and wild horses rambling over North America's plains. There are also carnivores such as coyotes, foxes, snakes, and wolves. They slink through the 8-foot-tall (2.5-meter) grasses and ambush prey like skunks, mice, and prairie dogs.

Try This

Cozy up in your favorite reading nook with Laura Ingalls Wilder's classic novel *On the Banks of Plum Creek*. Read about the author's exciting adventures in a sod hut. Once, an ox tumbled through the roof!

Water Worlds

The protected Florida Everglades is an ecoregion called flooded grasslands. The Everglades sprawl over 8,000 square miles (20,000 square kilometers). This water world is called "the River of Grass," because sawgrass covers most of the flowing water and makes it difficult to see.

The endangered West Indian manatee makes its home in the Everglades during the cold winter months before it heads out to the ocean in the spring. Gentle and playful, manatees are slow swimmers, a characteristic that places these 1,000-pound (453-kilogram) marine mammals at risk for collisions with boats. Fortunately, areas of the Everglades are marked "No Wake Zones." Boaters have to slow down, keep their eyes peeled for manatees, and steer clear to keep the marine mammals safe.

Grass Roots Action

Grasses are well adapted to the blustery environment of wide-open spaces. With their supple stems, grasses easily bow when windy gusts sweep over them. Built to endure drought, grass leaves are slender to prevent water loss.

The roots of grasses extend deep into the dark soil, seeking out water supplies. The deep roots also prevent hungry herbivores from completely yanking the grasses out. And when wildfires burn the grasses above, the deep, hardy roots survive below. They launch **sprouts** out of the ground to start regrowth.

Adapted for Wide, Open Spaces

Ungulates are mammals with hooves, such as antelope, bison, and horses. Hooves are adaptations for tromping through tall grasses. Did you know that a hoof is actually an oversized toenail? It's a thorny and scaly sheath that protects the foot. Scientists believe grassland animals walked on their toes and developed long legs so they could outrun predators.

Life in wide-open spaces is perilous. Unlike creatures in forest biomes, grassland animals can't climb trees to escape predators. How have they adapted?

Earth's Explorers

Katharine Lee Bates wrote the poem "America the Beautiful," which became the unofficial national anthem of the United States. In 1893, Bates enjoyed a cross-country train trip from Massachusetts to Colorado. Along the way, she spied the beautiful wheat fields of Kansas. Those "amber waves of grain" inspired the poet. Soon afterwards, she ventured to the 14,000-foot-high (4.25-kilometer) summit of Colorado's Pike's Peak. To reach the top, Bates bounced along in a rustic wagon, rode a mule, and finally endured an arduous hike. When she finally completed her climb, the "purple mountain majesties" dazzled the poet. On the spot, she jotted a poem in celebration.

AMERICA THE BEAUTIFUL
By Katharine Lee Bates
(1859-1929)
O beautiful for spacious skies,
For amber waves of grain,
For purple mountain majesties
Above the fruited plain.
America! America!
God shed His grace on thee,
And crown thy good with brotherhood
From sea to shining sea.

Prairie dogs, native to North America, spend much of their time digging extensive burrows. When a predator such as a bobcat or badger slinks up, the prairie dog dashes below ground to safety.

Prairie dogs are **social** animals that live in bustling underground environments called towns. The cute little rodents make special visits to see their pals, and even greet them with a quick smooch.

Another burrowing grassland animal is the endangered pink fairy armadillo from Argentina. Its favorite food is ants, so it likes to build its burrows next to anthills. The pink fairy is named for its delicate rose coloring and is only 4 inches (10 centimeters) long, making it the smallest member of the armadillo family. With its sharp claws, armor plates, and stout tail, the pink fairy is an expert digger. Once it tunnels through the earth, the pink fairy uses its hind plate and tail to block the burrow opening.

Words to Know

sprouts: shoots that grow from plants.
ungulates: mammals with hooves.
social: describes animals that prefer to live in groups, rather than by themselves.

DID YOU KNOW?

The pink fairy armadillo produces sounds like a wailing baby!

Threats to Grasslands

One of the biggest threats to grasslands is natural wildfires. But humans cause problems, too. Because grasslands are flat and fertile, they're perfect for farming and grazing. Yet both activities deplete the biome, especially when the grazing is excessive. And when people plow too much during the dry season, they make the land vulnerable to dust storms.

Make Your Own
TORNADO IN A BOTTLE

Do you live in Tornado Alley? That's the nickname of the central Great Plains region of the United States. Its geography is ripe for tornado activity. Find Tornado Alley on the map. South of the Great Plains lie the deserts of the Southwest where hot, dry air forms. The Gulf of Mexico, where warm, humid **air masses** develop, is to the southeast. In the Rocky Mountains to the west, cold, dry air forms.

April, May, and June are peak tornado months. During that time, the warm, humid air becomes trapped beneath the hot, dry air and the cold, dry air. Visualize a heavy lid hovering over the air. Imagine pressure building like water boiling in a pot. When the warm, humid air finally blasts free, it causes explosive thunderstorms. A twister twirls through the sky and touches ground, causing great destruction. You can make your own tornado in a bottle and watch a **vortex** develop.

■ **Tornado Alley**

Supplies

- water
- two, 2-liter plastic bottles
- dish detergent
- food coloring
- glitter
- flat metal washer about 1 inch in diameter with a ³/₈-inch (9.5 millimeter) hole
- duct tape

DID YOU KNOW

The United States is the tornado capital of the world. In an average year, about 1,200 tornadoes twist through the country.

1 Pour water into one of the 2-liter bottles until it's approximately two-thirds full. Add three squirts of dish detergent. Then add three drops of the food coloring. That will make the vortex "pop" visually. Add a dash of glitter to represent items from the ground that get sucked up into the vortex.

2 Place the flat metal washer on top of the filled bottle. Then turn the empty plastic bottle upside down. Place it on top of the washer so the two bottles are connected, with the empty bottle on top. Use duct tape to tightly secure the bottles.

3 Turn over the connected bottles so the full bottle is on top. Place the bottles on a steady flat surface or table. You should notice that water dribbles from the top bottle, through the drain hole, to the bottom. At the same time, air bubbles from the bottom bottle rise into the top one.

4 Holding both bottles, swirl them in a clockwise circle. Do you see rotating water in the top bottle? Does a funnel shape develop when the top bottle drains more rapidly? Voilà! That's the vortex.

5 How does the vortex form? As you rotate the water, **centripetal forces** draw it toward the center of the bottle. Gravity tugs the water to the drain hole. These two actions occur at the same time. When water drains into the bottom bottle, the vortex develops.

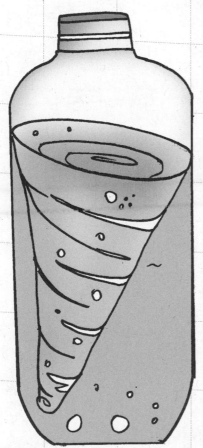

Words to Know

> **air mass:** a body of air that spreads over a wide area.
> **vortex:** a rapidly whirling spiral of air or water.
> **centripetal forces:** forces that pull a moving object toward a center area.

Make Your Own
CORN HUSK DOLL

Corn husk dolls were popular with both Native American and settler children. To craft the dolls, kids used corn husks, an abundant grassland product. Husks are the outer protective coverings around corn.

Next time you shuck corn, don't toss away the husks. Instead, create a doll—or two. Follow the directions to make a boy and a girl.

Supplies

- dried corn husks
- a tub or large flat pan of water
- towel
- twine
- scissors
- paints (optional)
- paint brushes (optional)
- fabric scraps (optional)

1 Allow the husks to dry in the sun for several days until they fade to a lighter color. Then soak them in the pan of water for about 15 minutes to soften them. They should be flexible to the touch. Gently pat them dry with the towel. Carefully pull the husks apart until you have at least 10 pieces for each doll. You might want extra pieces in case some get tattered.

2 Compare the sizes of the husks, and select four that are about the same length and width. Place them on top of one another in a pile. Then use the twine to tie the ends together. Position the twine close to the top. This tied bundle will become the doll's body.

3 Hold two of the husks in each hand. Fold them over the string, making certain that the string remains tucked inside. This folded area will become the doll's head. Circle twine just below the head and tie it.

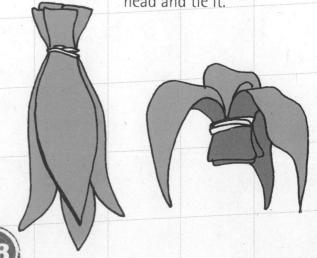

4 You're ready to make the arms. Select three long husks and run your fist over each to flatten it. Use the scissors to cut the pointy end on each so that it becomes straight. Then braid the three pieces together and tie each end with the twine.

5 Position the braided piece below the head, in between the husks of the body. Make sure that one arm juts out from either side of the body. You may have to reposition the braided piece to make the arms even.

6 Now pinch the body husks to create a waist for the doll. Tie the twine around the waist and below the arms. The twine will keep the arms positioned and keep them from sliding down.

7 Select another husk, and use your fist to flatten it. Wrap it around the back of the doll's neck, and cross it over the chest. This will form shoulders. Tie this husk to the doll over the twine at its waist.

8 It's time to create the legs. Hold the body husks below the doll's waist, and separate them into two legs. You might have to carefully split them from the bottom. Use the twine to tie off ankles at the bottom of the legs to make a doll wearing pants. If you prefer, you can make a dress by letting the main body husks hang free, untied. Use strands of husks to cover the twine.

9 Allow your doll to dry. Traditionally, dolls had no face. If you prefer, you can paint a face on the doll, and use fabric scraps for clothes.

DID YOU KNOW?

An average ear of corn contains a total of 800 kernels in 16 rows. Can you figure out how many kernels are in each row?

Make Your Own
Sss-soft Pretzel Sss-snakes

With no limbs and elongated bodies, snakes are able to slither through dense grasses and into burrows to catch prey. They can also move quickly to escape predators. Their coloring allows them to blend in with grassy surroundings.

For this project, you may want to start by researching different species of grassland snakes, such as the Butler's garter snake, the smooth green snake, the brown snake, and the fox snake. Study photos of the reptiles in their habitats. Then, use the pictures as a springboard for your creativity as you design your own snake pretzels!

Supplies

large mixing bowl	2 tablespoons sugar	large pot
wooden spoon	1 tablespoon salt	non-stick spray
measuring cups	food coloring (optional)	slotted spoon
measuring spoons	2½ to 3 cups unbleached all-purpose flour	large baking sheet
2 teaspoons instant yeast		egg glaze: 1 egg combined with 1 tablespoon water
2 cups water at room temperature	electric mixer	
	floured board	sesame seeds or coarse salt
3 cups King Arthur's 100% White Whole Wheat Flour	6 cups water	mustard (optional)
	2 tablespoons baking soda	stove and oven

Makes approximately 12 snakes

1 Use clean hands to handle supplies and ingredients. In the large mixing bowl, combine the yeast, 2 cups water, white whole wheat flour, sugar, and salt. If you'd like to color your snake, add a few drops of food coloring. Slowly add some unbleached flour, and mix until you have achieved a soft dough. The dough should not be sticky.

2 Remove the dough from the bowl and place it on the floured board. Knead the dough thoroughly. Then place it back in the bowl, and allow it to rise until it has doubled in size.

3 Once the dough has doubled, divide it into 12 pieces of approximately the same size. Roll each piece between your fingers to form a snake.

4 Measure 6 cups of water into the large pot. Add the baking soda and bring the water to a boil. In the meantime, coat the baking sheet with non-stick spray and preheat the oven to 450 degrees Fahrenheit (230 degrees Celsius).

5 When the water boils, place 4 snakes at a time into the pot. Allow them to boil for 1 minute. Then carefully remove them with the slotted spoon and place them on the cooking sheet.

JUST FOR LAUGHS

Q: What's the rattlesnake's favorite subject in school?

A: Hiss-story!

6 When you have boiled all the snakes and placed them on the sheet, coat each snake with egg glaze. Lightly drizzle seeds or salt over each.

7 Bake for 12 to 15 minutes. Serve the pretzels warm, or allow them to cool if you prefer. Depending on which snakes you created, you might choose to paint mustard stripes or patterns on them.

DID YOU KNOW?

To smell, snakes rapidly flick their forked tongues in and out of their mouths to detect odors.

Chapter 7

TROPICAL SAVANNAS

Tropical savannas are grasslands located near the equator, where it's hot all year. In this biome, temperatures rarely fall below 64 degrees Fahrenheit (18 degrees Celsius). The average temperature is about 80 degrees Fahrenheit (27 degrees Celsius), although it can spike to 100 degrees Fahrenheit (38 degrees Celsius).

Tropical savannas stretch over portions of Australia, India, South America, and major areas of Africa. In fact, Africa contains most of the planet's savannas. You'll find patchy expanses of lemon grass, red oats grass, and star grass here. While temperate grasslands are nearly treeless, you'll notice that scattered shrubs and trees rise above the grasses of the savanna.

Unlike the desert, African savannas feature wondrous biodiversity. Ferocious carnivores, such as cheetahs, leopards, and lions, top the food chain. They hunt hoofed herbivores, including impalas and wildebeests.

Overhead, hawks benefit from a birds-eye view of smaller prey, including meerkats, reptiles, and rodents, as they scurry through the grasses. Vultures swoop out of the sky to gorge on reeking **carrion**, while hippos stay cool, despite the scorching sun, by splashing in the river. Endangered elephant calves stick close to their mothers, whose mammoth bodies shade their babies as they munch on shrubs.

DID YOU KNOW?

Vultures are sloppy eaters. They like to dive right into gooey carrion. Good thing the messy birds have bald heads! Otherwise their feathers would get mussed.

Grassland or Desert?

Some people describe savannas as a combination of grasslands and deserts. That's because there are only two seasons, and they're both very different. For 6 to 8 months during the summer, fierce rains bombard the savanna. Luckily, the soil is porous, so it drains quickly. But it causes an astonishing rush of growth.

After the rainy season, the weather changes dramatically, becoming very dry. Drought transforms the landscape. Soil becomes crusty and cracked. In the dry season, lightning often strikes the savanna and ignites fires, which are quickly spread across the parched grasses by violent winds. Fire and scarce water make plant growth nearly impossible. Fires don't damage roots though, which remain protected underground. When the rainy season returns, the cycle of life begins anew.

JUST FOR LAUGHS

Q: What did the nice lightning bolt say to the naughty one?
A: You're shocking, but I always get such a charge out of you!

DID YOU KNOW?

Some savannas receive about 50 inches (127 centimeters) of rainfall during their wet seasons. If the rainfall was spread out over the course of an entire year, many savannas would transform into tropical rainforests!

Savanna Adaptations

Flora and fauna are well adapted to the harsh conditions in the savannas. For example, grass roots dig deep into the ground, and are protected by the soil during fires. They grow back quickly to provide food for the animals.

How do trees survive raging wildfires? Some have **fire-resistant** trunks. Africa's baobab tree, for example, boasts an immense spongy trunk. During the rainy season, it soaks up water and stashes it away for the impending drought. With its thick, crinkly folds, the baobab's trunk is well-protected against fierce flames. On top of that, the baobab only sprouts leaves during the rainy season.

Speaking of leaves, the acacia tree has some delicious ones. But they're high up near the top of these umbrella-like trees. The only animal that can reach them are giraffes, nature's tallest animals. These long-necked mammals, with their prehensile tongues, are well-adapted to nibble sky-high greens. Lower down, sharp thorns on the trunk ward off other hungry herbivores.

Halfway around the world, the savanna of the Australian Outback is full of animals that can survive on very little water, such as wallabies and kangaroos. With their brawny hind legs, kangaroos can leap 30 feet (9 meters) and move at 20–30 miles (32–48 kilometers) per hour, the speed cars travel on many city streets. Sounds exhausting, but kangaroos actually use very little energy when they hop because of the large tendons in their legs. Their jumbo feet aren't just for hopping, either. When a kangaroo senses danger, it sounds the alarm by thump-thump-thumping its feet on the ground.

JUST FOR LAUGHS

Q: How do you know a hungry hippo grazed in your fridge?
A: You discovered hoof prints in the butter!

Adapted for Safety

Grazing animals in wide-open spaces are easy targets for predators. What survival strategies do they use? Some, like zebras, find safety in numbers. When a herd of zebra gallops together, their famous black-and-white stripes blend together into one mass. A bewildered lion can't tell one zebra from another.

Others, such as giraffes, gazelles, and antelopes use their long legs to quickly sprint away from roaring lions, wild dogs, and fires. It's hard to outrun the cheetah, though. The speediest land mammal in the world, the spotted cheetah dashes at 70 miles (113 kilometers) per hour. That's faster than the speed limit on many highways!

Words to Know

carrion: the dead and rotting body of an animal.
fire-resistant: something that doesn't burn.

Symbiosis: A Win-Win Situation

Life in an ecosystem isn't just about predators and prey. There's plenty of cooperation, too, through **symbiosis**. Symbiosis occurs when animals or plants of differing species interact in partnerships that are beneficial for both. It's a win-win situation!

For example, hummingbirds get delicious nectar from flowers, but they return the favor by **pollinating**. And if you crawl on your belly to peek through the savanna brush, you might observe this odd couple: a red-billed oxpecker perched between an antelope's curved horns. As the antelope grazes, so does the bird—by plucking pesky parasites, ticks, and flies right from the herbivore's head! In a relationship that benefits both animals, the oxpecker scarfs up fast food while the antelope enjoys a speedy grooming.

The Nile crocodile and the spur-winged plover, a bird with spindly legs, are another coosome twosome. To beat the savanna heat when basking in the sun, the croc unhinges its cavernous mouth. It's an adaptation called **gaping**. That's just the wide open opportunity the plover needs to drop in for dinner. The plover alights between the fearsome predator's jaws. From its precarious perch, the plover digs out parasites and nibbles tasty tidbits of leftover meat trapped between the crocodile's pointy teeth. The croc, meanwhile, gets a nice teeth cleaning!

word exploration

The Greek translation of the word *symbiosis* is "living together."

JUST FOR LAUGHS

Q: What's black and white and red all over?
A: An embarrassed zebra!

Words to Know

symbiosis: a relationship between two different species of organisms in which each gains benefits from the other.
pollinating: transferring pollen from the male parts of the plant to the female parts.
gaping: an adaptation in which a crocodile opens its mouth to regulate heat.
poaching: illegal hunting or fishing.

JUST FOR LAUGHS

Q: In which year was the kangaroo born?

A: Leap year!

DID YOU KNOW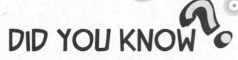

An elephant's trunk has about 40,000 muscles! The entire human body only has 640. The trunk is a flexible, multi-purpose tool. It grasps, smells, and tastes. It can also suck up and shoot out water like a hose. And that's not all. Itchy eye? The nimble trunk scratches it. Thirsty? The trunk sucks up water and spritzes it into the mouth.

Threats to the Savanna

One of the greatest risks to the savanna is **poaching**, or illegal hunting. Poaching can lead to extinction. The savanna contains many endangered animals. Although laws protect these animals, some people disobey the law so they can make money. For example, elephants are hunted for their valuable ivory tusks. Sometimes hunters set fire to the savanna to make it easier to spot their prey.

Desertification also threatens savannas. When people farm incorrectly, fertile lands can become battered and dry. Climate change leads to desertification as well. Overgrazing is another threat. It can reduce the amount of vegetation for wildlife to munch on.

Water Worlds

Billabong is an Australian English word. A billabong is a stagnant, or inactive, pool of water that develops during rainy seasons in the tropical savanna. Sometimes called an oxbow lake because if its u-shape, a billabong can also develop and remain behind as a dead-end when a river changes its course. A billabong branches into a larger waterway, usually a creek or a meandering river.

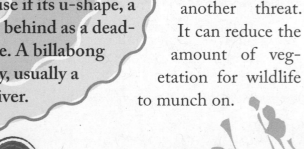

Bake Your Own
HONEY WHEAT BREAD

One of the world's most popular grains, wheat grows in the fertile soils of grasslands. It also grows in savannas, along with cotton, sugar cane, and **sorghum**. Whip up this delicious bread with whole wheat flour.

Supplies

2 large mixing bowls
measuring cups
measuring spoons
wooden spoon
½ cup water, 110 degrees Fahrenheit (43 degrees Celsius)
two packages yeast
2 cups fat-free milk
small pot

¼ cup butter
⅓ cup honey
¼ cup brown sugar
2½ teaspoons salt
½ cup wheat germ (optional)
2 tablespoons wheat gluten (optional)
3 cups whole wheat flour, divided

4 cups bread flour, divided
electric mixer
floured board
non-stick spray
clean dish towels
rolling pin
two 9-by-5-inch bread baking pans
melted butter and brush

Makes two loaves, approximately 16 slices per loaf

1 Use clean hands to handle supplies and ingredients. In the large mixing bowl, dissolve the yeast in the water by stirring with the wooden spoon. Allow the yeast to stand for 10 minutes.

Words to Know

sorghum: an important cereal crop grown in tropical areas, often used to feed livestock.

2 In the meantime, warm the milk in the pot until it reaches 110 degrees Fahrenheit (43 degrees Celsius) or a low simmer. With the wooden spoon, stir in the butter, honey, brown sugar, and salt. Pour the mixture into the large mixing bowl containing the yeast.

3 Add the wheat germ and wheat gluten if you're including them. Add 2 cups of the whole wheat flour, and 3 cups of the bread flour. With the electric mixer, beat the mixture for 3 full minutes.

4 Stir in the rest of the whole wheat flour, and add as much bread flour as you need to make a sticky dough. Place the dough on the floured board. Knead it for 10 full minutes until the dough becomes smooth and elastic.

5 Spray the second mixing bowl with the non-stick spray. Place the dough in the bowl, then turn it over so the top is coated with spray. Cover the dough with the dish towel. Allow it to rise in a warm place for about 75 minutes, until it has doubled in size.

6 Punch down the dough. Let it stand for 10 minutes. Then divide the dough in two. Use the rolling pin to shape each hunk of dough into a 9-inch-by-14-inch (23-by-35-centimeter) rectangle. Begin at the short end and tightly roll the dough. Pinch the ends to seal them.

7 Spray the loaf pans with non-stick spray. Then place one loaf of dough in each. Cover each with a dish towel. Allow them to rise in a warm place for one hour. Preheat the oven to 375 degrees Fahrenheit (190 degrees Celsius).

8 Bake for about 35 minutes or until the bread sounds hollow when you gently tap it with your fingers. If you prefer the bread to remain golden brown, cover it with foil for the last 15 minutes of baking. Otherwise, the crust will darken.

9 Remove the loaves from the pans and brush with butter. Allow them to cool before serving or storing.

JUST FOR LAUGHS

Q: What did the butter say to the bread?

A: I knead you!

Create Your Own
LIGHTNING

Dazzling bolts of lightning, which hit tall trees and ignite fires, are natural threats to savannas. Lightning forms inside thunderclouds, where small pieces of ice tumble in the air and bang into one another. Their collisions create electrical charges, which collect in the clouds.

Positive charges gather in a cloud's upper area, while negative charges accumulate in lower areas. On the ground, opposites attract. A positive charge develops on land beneath the storm, and lightning flashes down through the sky. That's called cloud-to-ground lightning.

Let's make lightning! In this activity, you'll represent the earth's surface. The pot will act as a thundercloud, while the fork becomes a lightning rod.

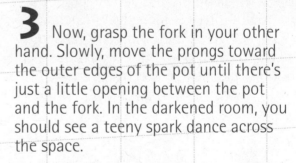

Supplies

- masking tape
- plastic dry cleaning bag or sheet
- flat surface
- dark room
- rubber gloves
- large iron or steel pot with a plastic handle
- iron or steel fork

1 Tape the dry cleaning bag or plastic sheet over a flat surface or tabletop. Draw the curtains and turn off the lights to make the room as dark as possible. Slip on the rubber gloves.

2 Grip the pot by its plastic handle. Place it on the plastic sheet, press down, and rub it energetically over the surface.

3 Now, grasp the fork in your other hand. Slowly, move the prongs toward the outer edges of the pot until there's just a little opening between the pot and the fork. In the darkened room, you should see a teeny spark dance across the space.

Hints: Do this activity when it's cool and dry, not humid. Don't use an aluminum pot, or it won't work. And be sure you keep the gloves on! Like the plastic handle on the pot, rubber is an insulator and doesn't conduct electricity.

Chapter 8

TUNDRA

Make sure you bundle up when you explore Earth's frostiest biome, the tundra. Here, biodiversity is low, soil is poor, and rainfall is scarce—less than 10 inches (25 centimeters) per year. The tundra experiences only two seasons, winter and summer. Winters are bitterly cold, with temperatures plummeting to -40 degrees Fahrenheit (-40 degrees Celsius), while summers warm only to about 64 degrees Fahrenheit (18 degrees Celsius).

Did you know there are three areas of tundra: alpine, Arctic, and Antarctic? This treeless biome is one big frosty circle at the top of the planet and on top of tall mountain peaks. The tundra covers about 14 percent of Earth's landmass in the northern Arctic areas of Alaska, Canada, Greenland, and Siberia. These regions in the Northern Hemisphere are called the Arctic tundra.

Located on mountains above the **timberline** where no trees grow, is the alpine tundra. It's not only in the Northern Hemisphere that you'll shiver in the tundra. Although most of Antarctica is considered a dry desert, a stretch of tundra is present along its coasts. Fittingly, it's known as the Antarctic tundra.

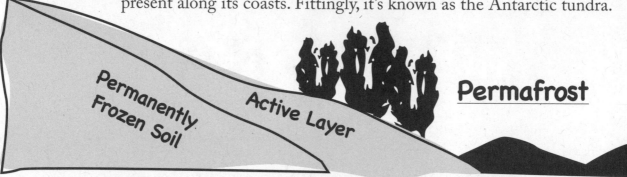

Permanently Frozen Soil

Active Layer

Permafrost

What characterizes the tundra? **Permafrost**. It's exactly what it sounds like! A layer of permanently frozen subsoil just beneath the surface of the ground. You won't encounter permafrost in warmer biomes. In the summer months, when the weather warms up, the top layer, or **active layer**, of the permafrost thaws. The rest, however, remains frozen. It never defrosts. When the active layer melts, it supplies a rich ecosystem for animals, plants, and insects. Then as winter approaches again, the active layer refreezes.

Unfortunately, as the earth's temperatures rise, the thaw depth increases. Decomposing materials release more **carbon dioxide** into the atmosphere, and the greenhouse effect gets stronger.

DID YOU KNOW?

The North Pole has no real land—it's just a colossal slab of ice!

Seed Vault

In 2008 a team of scientists in Norway created a very special storage vault by chiseling into a frigid Arctic mountain's permafrost. This global food bank stores representative plant seeds from the world's precious supply. It protects the earth's plants in case of catastrophe, such as disease or the effects of continued global warming. The seed vault already holds samples of 208,000 plants from across the planet. It's large enough to stockpile 2 billion of the world's seeds. Permafrost will safeguard the seeds, even if the climate continues to warm.

Adapted for Extremely Short Growing Seasons

You've already learned that plants are the primary producers of the food chain. Without plants, animals can't survive. In the Arctic tundra, plants have to deal with an extremely short growing season—the shortest on the planet, in fact. It's only about 50 days long, shorter than a summer break from school.

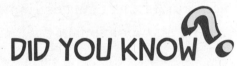

DID YOU KNOW

Penguins plop onto their bellies to slide over icy snow! Can you tell why this sliding is called tobogganing? Wheeee!

With chilly soil and not much time to grow and carry out photosynthesis, how do plants do what they need to do? Many plants, such as grasses, lichens, mosses, and shrubs, stay small. They hug the ground to avoid bitter winds. Close to the ground, short plants also absorb the sun's heat, which radiates from the soil.

DID YOU KNOW

The Inuit people of the Arctic eat the purple saxifrage's sweet, star-shaped blossoms.

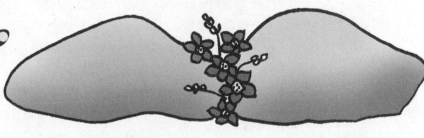

For example, the purple saxifrage flower of Denali, Alaska, is adapted for its inhospitable environment. One of the first tundra flowers to bloom when temperatures heat up, it often makes its cheery appearance as the snow melts. A cushion plant, the saxifrage grows in a ground-hugging cluster that looks like a pillow. It sets down deep roots in crevices between rocks, which absorb the sun's energy.

Words to Know

timberline: also called the treeline—the elevation or limit beyond which trees do not grow in mountains or northern latitudes.

permafrost: permanently frozen subsoil and rock just beneath the surface of the ground.

active layer: the layer of soil that melts in the summer.

carbon dioxide: a greenhouse gas that contributes to climate change and global warming.

Adapted for Bitterly Cold Temperatures

Many animals avoid the frigid Arctic winters, when food is scarce, by migrating south to warmer climates. Immense herds of lichen-loving caribou move to forest biomes. Other animals, such as the singing vole, which earned its name because of the shrill noise it makes when it spots predators, thrive in the subnivian layer. There they can nibble on roots and stems. Some animals hibernate, like the Arctic ground squirrel and the grizzly bear.

Many animals stay outside and brave the elements. Have you ever bundled up in a puffy winter jacket on a freezing day? It insulates you against wicked winds and frosty temperatures. For animals, **blubber** does the same thing. Blubber is a thick layer of fat located just beneath the skin that provides insulation for tundra dwellers.

You've probably also swaddled yourself in a woolly scarf and hat to go outside and play in the snow. For tundra animals, woolly coats are essential.

Words to Know

blubber: an insulating layer of fat underneath an animal's skin, that helps keep the animal warm.

glacier: an enormous mass of frozen snow and ice that moves across the earth's surface.

Walrus Blubber

An adult walrus weighs anywhere between 882 and 3,748 pounds (400 and 1,700 kilograms)! Calves weigh from 99 to 156 pounds (45 to 70 kilograms) at birth. A 6-inch (15-centimeter) layer of blubber protects the walrus and contributes to its bulky body mass. Yet blubber is not the only adaptation on which walruses rely. Its two hanging tusks act as built-in pick-axes. Walruses stab their tusks into the ice to hoist themselves out of the water and to haul their blubbery bodies over their rocky, icy habitat.

Polar bears, seals, and walruses depend on blubber and woolly coats to protect them against the cold, both on the land and in the water.

Bigger bodies, shorter legs, and smaller ears is a combination that helps Arctic mammals and birds survive. Compare, for instance, the Arctic rabbit with the jackrabbit of the desert biome. Instead of oversized ears that allow heat to escape like the jackrabbit's, the Arctic hare has short ears to conserve heat. A gray color in the summer, the Arctic hare turns white in the winter to camouflage itself against the snowy environment. The Arctic fox, ermine, and willow ptarmigan do the same thing.

Threats to the Tundra

Oil drilling in the tundra causes air, land, water, and noise pollution. The racket disrupts wildlife and sends animals fleeing in search of peace and quiet. Oil spills are disastrous, ruining the environment and killing animals on land and in the water.

word exploration

The word *tundra* comes from the Finnish word *tunturia*, which means "treeless plain."

Climate change has impacted the Arctic more than any other place on the planet. The earth's higher temperatures cause Arctic ice to melt and **glaciers** to shrink. Polar bears can't find enough food to survive. Thin and unhealthy, mother polar bears can't produce enough milk to feed their young. Many bears attempt to swim great distances in search of food and new habitats. Sadly, some drown in the process.

DID YOU KNOW ?

In the summer of 2008, people in Iceland spotted polar bears that had ventured 200 miles (322 kilometers) from their home turf to hunt for seals. It's a sign that climate change has caused the endangered predators to roam greater distances in search of food.

In 2008 the United States Government named the polar bear an endangered species. There's a real possibility that this symbol of the Arctic could become extinct in your lifetime.

word exploration

In the 1950s, U.S. Air Force pilots who were stationed in Alaska complained about the sky's smoggy conditions. When the haze hovered in the air during flight missions, the pilots' **visibility** dropped. J. Murray Mitchell, an Air Force **meteorologist**, coined the term "Arctic Haze" in 1956 to describe the air conditions.

How can you help? Try to cut down on your greenhouse gas emissions. Instead of riding in a car, hop on your bike or roll on your skateboard. Take the bus or organize a carpool among your friends.

DID YOU KNOW

The Arctic tern has plenty to crow about! This 2-pound bird has a white body, black head, and orange feet. It also migrates the longest-distance of any bird—21,750 miles (35,000 kilometers) over the sea from the Arctic to Antarctica and back again! That's roughly the earth's entire circumference! How long does this perilous flight from the top of the world to the bottom take? About 3 months.

Tundra Team

What's it like to play football on the frozen tundra? Ask the Barrow Whalers, a high school team in Barrow, Alaska, the northernmost town in the United States. The Whalers' field is right alongside the Arctic Ocean. With that location, is it any wonder that in 2008 a polar bear wandered near the field to take a peek at the team?

Hardy spectators cheer the Whalers—until these fans start to freeze. Then they duck into school bus warming stations circled like wagons to block the field from Arctic blasts of wind.

Science in Action!
Meet Nick Longo, Environmental Scientist

One of the planet's most notorious environmental disasters occurred on a chilly March day in 1989. A tanker called the *Exxon Valdez,* transporting 53 million gallons (208 million liters) of oil from the Alaska Pipeline, ran aground on Bligh Reef in Alaska's Prince William Sound. The ship ruptured its **hull** on the jagged rocks of the reef, and dumped nearly 11 million gallons (42 million liters) of **crude oil** into the Sound's pristine water. According to NOAA, the National Oceanic and Atmospheric Administration, that's enough oil to fill 430 classrooms!

The oil rapidly spread across the Sound and oozed over shorelines. It floated on the surface of the water and covered cormorants and murrelets, seabirds that inhabit the region. Oily waters poisoned whales, bears, and salmon.

The Coast Guard, Exxon responders, and emergency teams sprang into action. Environmental scientists and workers rushed to hose down blackened beaches and capture the oil in **booms**, which are floating barriers. Meet Nick Longo, an environmental scientist who worked at the site.

BIOMES: Tell us about your experiences as a first responder after the oil spill.

DID YOU KNOW?

The willow ptarmigan is Alaska's state bird. How does this feather-footed member of the grouse family tackle winter? It dive-bombs into a mound of powdery snow to keep warm and to duck out of predators' view. Plunging into its shelter from above means the bird leaves no telltale tracks.

Words to Know

visibility: the distance someone can see during certain weather conditions.

meteorologist: someone who studies the earth's atmosphere and forecasts the weather.

hull: a ship's body.

crude oil: liquid petroleum that is extracted from the ground, but not yet transformed into gasoline, engine oil, diesel oil, kerosene, and other petroleum-based products.

boom: a floating barrier used to contain oil spilled in water.

hypothermia: a dangerous condition caused by exposure to cold where body temperatures plunge to levels that are life-threatening.

NICK LONGO: I was on one of the first ships released into the harbor. On my first ride out to the site we stopped the boat to allow five whales to cross in front of us! Our job was to protect sensitive harbors in Prince William Sound. Over a period of four weeks, we stretched oil-spill control booms, which are like puffy plastic curtains, across the mouths of harbors and river deltas. The booms kept the oil from washing in with the tides and impacting shorelines.

JUST FOR LAUGHS

Q: Who is the Emperor penguin's favorite relative?

A: Aunt Arctica!

DID YOU KNOW

How many gallons of oil do people across the globe consume each day? About 85 million barrels. At 42 gallons per barrel, that's 3,570 million gallons a day (13,514 million liters)!

BIOMES: What was the tundra weather like?

NICK LONGO: Extremely cold. If we toppled into the water, we had just three minutes to scramble out or we'd freeze and **hypothermia** would set in. We wore insulated coveralls that doubled as flotation devices, insulated gloves, stocking caps, and hoods. And thermal undies.

BIOMES: How did the spill impact animals?

NICK LONGO: Some animals were able to stay below the floating oil. The worst situation occurred when animals became coated with oil. Slick oil covered skin, fur, and feathers. Animals' natural abilities to fly and to remain insulated and waterproof failed, so some froze to death or drowned. Sea birds, harbor seals, and otters tried to lick themselves clean—and sadly swallowed toxic oil in the process. When we spotted sea otters covered with oil, we immediately notified another clean-up group, who hurried to wash them. We worked at the spill site for a full month, 24/7. A day-tour boat was our main mode of transportation, and it was our lodging as well.

BIOMES: What's the coolest part of your job? What tip can you offer to kids?

NICK LONGO: It's exciting to protect the environment for the good of all living things. Take a bike ride or walk through your own environment. See what you can do to protect it. Pick up litter. Or beautify an area by planting a tree. Just get out there and experience the sights, sounds, and smells of your environment!

Test Your AIR QUALITY

Arctic Haze is not a new rock band. It's a specific polar air mass. Chock-full of chemical pollutants from Canada, Eurasia, and the United States, this reddish-brown smog hangs over Alaska. When too little precipitation falls to wash it away, Arctic Haze parks itself in the sky, creating poor air quality.

What's the air quality like where you live? Conduct this test to find out.

1 Choose four separate areas, both indoors and outdoors, to test the air. Indoors you might select your kitchen, and outdoors target a bush or shrub. Jot each location on a separate sheet of your journal, for example, "On the Kitchen Windowsill" or "Next to the Azalea Bush." You'll record observations under these headings in Step 4.

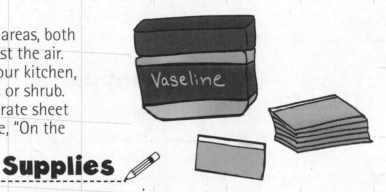

Supplies

- journal and pencil
- index cards
- permanent maker
- craft stick
- petroleum jelly
- magnifying glass

2 With the marker, label one index card for each location. Your labels should match those in your journal. Then use the craft stick to spread petroleum jelly over the cards. Leave each card in a safe spot in its target area. Wait 8 hours.

3 You're ready to collect data. Visit each location to gather its card. Use the magnifying glass to study each sample. Do you observe any particles? What color are they? Can you identify what they are? Record your findings in your journal.

4 While you're at each location, use your senses to take in your surroundings. In your journal, write your observations and descriptions of the area. Can you smell anything? Does the air feel dusty or damp? Do you see blowing sand or plant parts? Are man-made conditions such as cigarette smoke, industrial emissions, or road construction affecting air quality? How about a natural occurrence, such as blustery weather?

5 Place each sample in a row. Use the magnifying glass to compare and contrast each card. Which sample is the cleanest? The dirtiest? What conclusions can you draw about your air quality?

Make Your-Own
GLACIER

A glacier is a gargantuan mass of compacted snow and solid ice. Formed in the Arctic and Antarctic thousands of years ago, glaciers also develop outside these areas on mountain peaks and in valleys. As snow thaws and freezes again, glaciers thicken and continue to grow.

Slowly but continuously, glaciers move. In fact, people have called glaciers "rivers of ice" since they constantly move like water. As glaciers advance, or increase in size and move forward, they haul boulders and push mounds of rock debris in front of them. As they retreat, or melt, glaciers deposit boulders in new places. They create lakes, carve craggy hills, and etch valleys into the landscape.

1 With the scissors, carefully cut away one of the milk carton's side panels.

2 Fill about one-third of the milk carton with gravel, rocks, and sand to form rock debris. Pour in enough water to cover the rock debris, and stir with the wooden spoon. Place the milk carton into a freezer and allow it to freeze solid.

3 When the carton is completely frozen, remove it from the freezer. Fill another third of the carton with the same gravel, rocks, sand, and water mixture. Return the carton to the freezer, and allow it to freeze solid again. Your glacier will be growing larger and thicker.

Supplies

scissors	wooden spoon
half-gallon milk carton	freezer
gravel	wooden board or panel
rocks	12 feet (3.5 meters)
sand	long by 1 foot (0.30
water	meter) wide

Water Worlds

Kettle lakes, including those found in Alaska's Denali National Park and Preserve, are formed by glaciers. When glaciers retreat, mammoth chunks of ice stay behind, partially buried beneath sandy gravel. In time, the ice melts, and it leaves a large, bowl-shaped indentation in the sediment. Groundwater seeps into the hole and combines with precipitation to create a kettle lake.

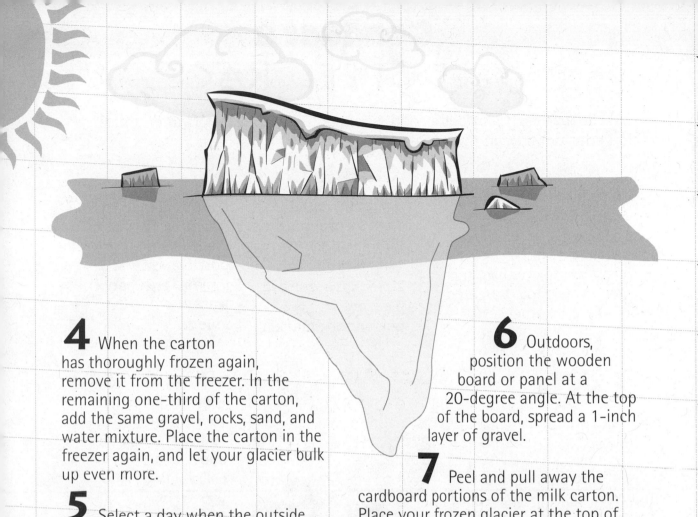

4 When the carton has thoroughly frozen again, remove it from the freezer. In the remaining one-third of the carton, add the same gravel, rocks, sand, and water mixture. Place the carton in the freezer again, and let your glacier bulk up even more.

5 Select a day when the outside temperature is above 55 degrees Fahrenheit (13 degrees Celsius) and below 80 degrees Fahrenheit (27 degrees Celsius). Now, you're ready to take your glacier outside and observe its movement.

6 Outdoors, position the wooden board or panel at a 20-degree angle. At the top of the board, spread a 1-inch layer of gravel.

7 Peel and pull away the cardboard portions of the milk carton. Place your frozen glacier at the top of the board. Wait about an hour.

8 Observe how the glacier has moved across the board. What happened to the gravel? How much ice has melted? Has any rock debris been left behind? What formations do you notice?

DID YOU KNOW

Like gigantic water jugs, the glaciers and ice caps in Antarctica and Greenland hold about 69 percent of the planet's freshwater supply. But climate change is speeding up the melting process. If all the earth's glaciers and ice sheets completely melted, sea levels would rise about 200 feet (61 meters)!

Conduct a
SEED SPEED RACE

How does freezing affect a seed's ability to **germinate**? Find out when you conduct a Seed Speed Race.

1 Tally the total number of seeds you have, and divide that number in half. Place half of the seeds in the ziplock freezer bag, and place the bag into a freezer. Set aside the other seeds and keep them at room temperature. Wait 24 hours.

2 With the marker, write "First Frozen" on one plastic tub or container. Write "Not Frozen" on the other. Fill each tub about halfway to the top with the potting soil. Place the frozen seeds in the soil of the first tub and the other seeds in the soil of the second tub. Then, add more soil until each tub or container is about three-quarters full.

3 Place the tubs of seeds next to each other in a sunny location. In your journal, hypothesize what will happen to the seeds. Do you think one set will germinate more quickly than the other? Why or why not?

Supplies ✏️

- fast-growing seeds, such as green beans, lima beans, or radishes
- ziplock freezer bag
- freezer
- permanent marker
- 2 empty clear plastic deli tubs or other containers
- potting soil
- journal and pencil
- water
- ruler

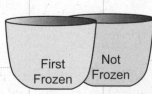

Potting Soil

4 Water—but don't drown—the seeds every day for 10 days. Notice their progress above and below the soil. Jot down your observations in your journal. Sketch the stages of growth you observe.

5 Which set of seeds, if either, won the Seed Speed Race? What conclusions can you draw about the effects of freezing on seeds?

First Frozen   Not Frozen

Words to Know 🔍

germinate: to begin to grow from a seed.

Chapter 9

MOUNTAINS

N ow let's climb up some steep and rocky mountains. Mountains soar high over every continent, covering 20 percent of the earth's land surface. They also rise from the floors of each of the planet's oceans.

Some scientists don't consider mountains a separate biome. Why? Because mountains contain other biomes. For example, the lower slopes of mountains often include waving grasslands or vast deserts. Deciduous forests often cover the foothills. As you **ascend**, you'll move through coniferous forests that bathe a mountain in lush green. Higher up, tundra landscapes above the treeline paint the peaks snowy white in winter, and sometimes all year long.

Water Worlds

Mountain waterfalls are breathtaking sights. Frothy waters cascade over rocky ledges and tumble into streams or rivers below. It takes thousands of years for a waterfall to form. Flowing waters encounter a rocky area of bedrock that doesn't wear away from erosion. This hard rock creates a steep platform from which waters vertically plunge.

DID YOU KNOW

The 2-ounce pygmy tarsier can fit in the palm of your hand. With its oversized eyes and ears, this teeny primate can swivel its head 180 degrees like an owl. Scientists believed the pygmy tarsier became extinct in 1921. Then in 2008 they were thrilled to encounter four live tarsiers in the mountains of Indonesia.

Despite this multi-ecoregion feature, some scientists do classify mountains as distinct biomes. They point out that certain wildlife, such as the Himalayan marmot, live only in particular mountain areas. As with other biomes, mountain ranges contain a variety of water ecosystems: ponds, streams, wetlands, rivers, and lakes.

Mountain Formation

Mountain ranges have formed through **geological events** over millions of years. The earth is made of rocky **plates** that constantly drift. When these plates crash into one another, the pressure causes some land to sink. Other land lifts, crinkles, or forms a **fault**. That's a crack in the earth's surface. When melted rock surges through the cracked areas, volcanic activities can occur. Over time, ice, water, and wind erosion carve out breathtaking, craggy landscapes.

Words to Know

ascend: climb, move upward.
geological events: earthquakes, volcanic eruptions, and erosion.
plates: sheets of drifting solid rock on the earth's surface.
fault: a crack in the earth's surface that can cause earthquakes.
elevation: height above sea level.

Life Zones

Climate, an important characteristic of biomes, varies in mountains. That's another reason not all scientists agree that mountains are a biome. As you climb higher and higher up a single mountain, you'll experience dropping temperatures.

The soil becomes different as you trudge up. You'll also spot changing vegetation and different animals.

Depending where you are in the world, you'll encounter different life zones on mountains. Life zones describe ecological communities and where they are located on mountains. **Elevation**, soil, levels of dryness or wetness, and types of vegetation all influence life zones.

In North America's Rocky Mountains, for example, the three main life zones are montane, subalpine, and alpine. The montane level is located below 8,000 feet (2,438 meters). It's the warmest and driest zone and is the most hospitable to people and wildlife. Aspen trees, blue spruce, Douglas firs, and lodgepole pines are common here.

You'll find the subalpine zone at an elevation of 8,000 to 11,500 feet (2,438 to 3,505 meters). Trees, mostly firs and spruces, are shorter and more scattered.

DID YOU KNOW?

Himalayan marmots, relatives of the woodchuck, live at mind-boggling altitudes of 10,000 to 14,000 feet (3,084 to 4,267 meters)! These grass-gnawing rodents have been nicknamed "whistle pigs" because they whistle shrilly to alert their pals when predators are snooping around.

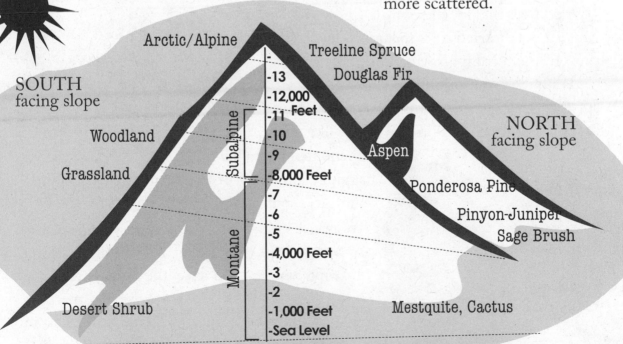

Rocky Mountain Life Zones with Elevations

The Giant Panda

In China, pandas are a symbol of peace—they're also the symbol of the World Wildlife Federation. The giant panda totters on the brink of extinction. Increasing human populations raise the need for usable land. Responding to this need, people have cleared away the panda's habitat to provide logs for fuel and land for rice farms. In doing so, they have also cleared away the bamboo plants that pandas feast on.

Towering above 11,500 feet (3,505 meters) is the alpine zone, where wildflowers and squat shrubs hug the ground. High winds and a short growing season make conditions difficult for plants.

Gnarled and Flagged

Just how difficult are the growing conditions? As you near the **Krummholz Line**, you'll observe twisty, gnarled trees that look like shrubs. Powerful winds cause these dwarfed trees to lurch sideways and prevent them from growing upright.

Although you might spot scattered tall spruce trees, you'll notice they only have branches and needles on one side—like a flag. This phenomenom, called flagging, is a result of the winds that constantly pummel the trees.

To survive in such harsh conditions, alpine plants are **perennials**, plants that live through several growing seasons. Because they are perennials, they don't have to expend precious energy to grow stems and leaves in one season, the way **annuals** do.

DID YOU KNOW?

The giant panda has an oily coating on its woolly fur. This adaptation is like a waterproof raincoat that keeps the panda warm in China's mountains.

word exploration

Krummholz comes from the German words krumm, which means "twisted," and Holz, for "wood."

DID YOU KNOW?

When llamas tussle, they screech and moan. Opponents spit goop, neck-wrestle, and wallop each other with their chests. Oh, the llama drama!

Adapted to the High Life

Are you feeling a little bit loopy up here? It's the air! Mountain air is thin and cold and contains little oxygen. The higher the elevation, the more challenging it becomes for animals to  survive. How are they adapted for the high life? Let three marvelous mountain mammals strut their stuff.

The pine marten of the Rocky Mountains is a member of the weasel family. This little predator sports a cat-like face and ears. It sprouts extra fur on its toe pads to keep its feet toasty as it scurries over snow. Remember the desert's fennec fox, which grows thick fur to shield its feet on scorching sands? This is a similar adaptation for surviving a different environment.

How does the threatened yak adapt to the thin air in the high altitudes of Asia's Himalayas? This shaggy member of the ox family boasts a burly chest with huge lungs that allow it to inhale hefty amounts of air. A fleecy outer coat and a downy inner one provide a double layer of protection against the unforgiving region, where temperatures can plunge to -40 degrees Fahrenheit (-40 degrees Celsius).

The terrain is also tricky. In the Andes of Peru, the sure-footed llama navigates treacherous terrain. Double-toed feet with leathery bottom pads prevent them from stumbling.

Words to Know

Krummholz Line: the highest elevation where krummholz trees grow.

krummholz: stunted trees growing just above the treeline on a mountain.

perennials: plants that flower and live for more than one season.

annual: plants that flower and die in one season. New ones grow the next year from seeds.

Earth's Explorers

The Inca Empire in Peru (1438-1533) depended on the fleecy llama for meat, wool, and transportation. Archaeologists have discovered beautiful silver and stone llama statues in Inca ruins.

Make Your Own
ERUPTING VOLCANO

When magma, or molten rock, busts through the earth's crust, it splits and cracks rocks. Fiery volcanoes erupt, spewing fountains of lava, toxic gases, and choking ash. Create your own volcano and experience its eruption!

Supplies

- 1 cup flour
- ½ cup salt
- 1 cup water
- 1 tablespoon cooking oil
- 2 teaspoons cream of tartar
- mixing bowl
- wooden spoon
- saucepan

- work surface
- aluminum foil
- cardboard paper towel tube
- ruler
- scissors
- masking tape
- thick cardboard, 12 inches by 12 inches (30 by 30 centimeters)

- newspaper
- tempera paints and paint brushes
- goggles
- baking soda
- red food coloring
- 1 cup (237 milliliters) vinegar

1 Make the modeling dough first. Add the first five items on the supply list to the mixing bowl, and stir with the wooden spoon. Then carefully pour the mixture into the saucepan. Over low heat, stir constantly until the mixture forms a thick dough.

2 Allow the dough to cool until it is safe to knead thoroughly. Roll the dough into a ball, and wrap it in the foil to keep it from drying out.

3 Now, ask an adult to help you cut the cardboard tube to about 8 inches (20 centimeters) in length. Use some of the modeling dough to plug one end of the tube.

4 Use the masking tape to fasten the tube, plugged side on the bottom, to the cardboard. Crinkle the newspaper into balls of different sizes.

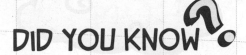

DID YOU KNOW?

Scientists have discovered fossils of seashells on Mt. Everest, the world's tallest mountain. How can that be? Because at one time, millions of years ago, the ocean covered the land where Everest now towers.

5 Tape the newspaper balls all around the tube and over the cardboard to shape a volcano. Place larger wads of paper at the bottom of the volcano and smaller ones at the top to form a cone shape.

6 Use the modeling dough to cover the volcano. Make sure to leave the top of the tube uncovered. Paint your volcano to look like a rocky volcano cone. Allow everything to dry overnight.

7 When the volcano is dry, slip on your goggles. Pour baking soda into the cardboard tube so that it's at least halfway full. Add a few drops of red food coloring into the vinegar so your molten lava will look authentic.

8 Now, take your volcano outside for the eruption. Wear your goggles as you pour the vinegar into the cardboard tube. Step away from the volcano, and watch it erupt!

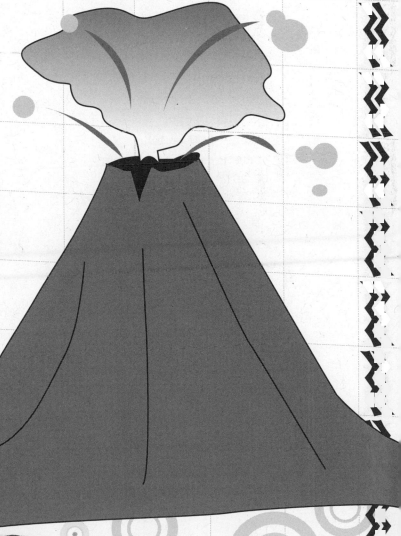

Experiment With
WATER EROSION

Erosion occurs naturally through the action of glaciers, water, and wind. It contributes to spectacular mountain scenery. Let's simulate erosion and watch nature's sculptor in action!

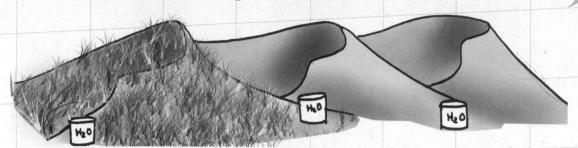

Supplies

sand

12 toothpicks

grass clippings or shredded paper

journal and pencil

watering can with water or hose with spray nozzle

1 Go outside and use the sand to create three little hills on a sidewalk, driveway, or paved area. Allow about 12 inches (30 centimeters) between each hill. Press the sand hills tightly on their sides, as if you're packing a snowball or mudball. Place four toothpicks in the sides of each hill.

2 Sprinkle the grass clippings or shredded paper over the first sand hill. Make sure the toothpicks are still peeking out. Leave the other two hills as they are.

3 Sketch and label each of the hills in your journal. Predict what will happen to the first two hills during a light rainfall. How will the grass or paper influence the outcome? What will happen to the toothpicks? Jot down your predictions.

4 Use the watering can to cause a light rainfall by sprinkling a small amount of water on the first and second sand hills. What happens to the toothpicks? How much sand flushes away? Do the grass clippings or shredded paper prevent erosion, slow it down, or speed it up?

5 You have a lone sand hill left. Predict what will happen to it in a heavy rainfall, and write down your prediction.

6 Now, use the sprinkling can or hose to create the rainfall. Pour a large amount of water on the sand hill. What happens to the toothpicks? How much sand flushes away? How does it compare to what happened to the previous two hills? What conclusions can you draw about your experiment?

Chapter 10

OCEANS

Y ou've learned about terrestrial biomes and the fresh waters found in them. Now, let's take a quick dip in the ocean or marine biome, the largest of all the biomes. Earth is a watery world. It's nicknamed the "Blue Planet" because water covers more than 71 percent of its surface.

Do you live near an ocean? The marine biome is the saltwater surrounding all the continents and includes the Arctic, Atlantic, Indian, Pacific, and Southern Oceans. Ocean waters never stop moving. Constant ocean motion is driven by the wind and by the earth's **rotation** as it spins on its **axis**.

DID YOU KNOW?

As the earth rotates, it spins from east to west.

Wind, which is moving air, starts with heat from the sun. As the sun's rays fall on the earth, they heat up the land, which in turn heats the air above it. Warm air rises. Cooler air over oceans moves in to take the place of the warm air as it rises. The shifting, moving air is the wind.

What kinds of winds are common where you live? **Prevailing winds** are those that ordinarily blow across a particular region. For example, trade winds prevail in the tropical zones along the equator. Trade winds always blow from east to west. In the middle latitudes of the temperate zone, the prevailing winds are called westerly winds. As their name indicates, westerlies blow from west to east.

Have you ever ridden a frothy wave? When wind blows over the ocean, it transfers energy to the water's surface and thrusts water away. The water changes shape, forming waves. Depending on the wind speed, wave size varies. A light breeze ruffles the ocean with gentle fingers, while a storm's powerful gusts create towering whitewater peaks.

Words to Know

rotation: turning around a fixed point.

axis: an imaginary line down the middle of a sphere around which it rotates.

prevailing wind: the most common wind in an area.

currents: constantly moving masses of water.

tsunami: an abnormally large, destructive wave caused by an underwater earthquake.

Try This

Make waves! Grab a small bowl and fill it halfway with water. Hold the bowl over a sink. Now, slowly blow over the water surface to create a light breeze. Those little ripples that result are called cats' paws. An old sailors' superstition claimed cats became frisky when gales brewed at sea, predicting that calm breezes would turn wild. Now, blast the water with a fast puff of breath. What happens to the waves?

Currents are masses of water that are always on the move. Surface ocean currents are caused by winds and by the earth's rotation. Currents move in a particular path, flowing in swirling motions. In earth's Northern Hemisphere, circular currents flow in a clockwise direction. What's clockwise? That's the direction a clock's minute and hour hands move. In the Southern Hemisphere, currents move counterclockwise, as if a clock's hands are traveling backward. Some scientists compare currents to streams or rivers within the ocean.

DID YOU KNOW

The world's tallest known wave clobbered Lituya Bay, Alaska, in 1958. A destructive **tsunami**, the wave towered at 1,750 feet (525 meters). Speaking of towers, that monster wave was higher than the Taipei 101 Tower. At 1,671 feet (509 meters), it's the world's second-tallest building.

Two Toothy Predators

Two predators at the top of the food chain, the barracuda and the shark, are adapted for hunting. Sleek and missile-shaped, the toothy twosome easily flit around the nooks and crannies of coral reefs. Barracudas use their eyes to spot prey, such as meaty tuna and grouper. They attack with a speedy strike. With two sets of jutting, triangular teeth, fierce barracudas snatch and devour the fish.

Known for their huge jaws, sharks prey on barracudas. Rather than using eyes to spot dinner, sharks sense their prey's vibrations in water and sneak up behind or beneath their victims. Sharks boast a remarkable mouthful of choppers, too. If a shark's tooth snaps off as it gnaws prey, it's no problem. A new tooth grows to replace the lost one.

Camouflage coloring is another shark adaptation. The carnivore's skin is darker on top of its body than on the bottom. Here's how it works. Unsuspecting prey darting above the predator peer down. The shark is camouflaged in darker waters—and it snags the prey. When prey swim under the predator, the shark's lighter-colored bottom camouflages it against bright, sunlight zone waters.

DID YOU KNOW

At a whopping 64 million square miles (166 million square kilometers), the Pacific is the largest ocean in the world. It's more than double the size of the Atlantic Ocean.

Salt Water

Have you ever swallowed a bit of ocean water? How did it taste? Over the course of millions of years, freshwater from rainfall, rivers, and streams washed over the earth's rocks. Some rocks have a lot of salt in them, and salt dissolves in water. The water washed the salt, a clear compound called **sodium chloride**, away from the rocks and into the sea. No wonder the ocean tastes salty—sodium chloride is used to make table salt.

Temperatures and Zones

Although the water of the marine biome is constantly moving and mixing, water temperatures still vary quite a lot depending on location. Polar waters, in the far north and south near the poles, are as low as a frosty 28 degrees Fahrenheit (-2 degrees Celsius). Tropical waters close to the equator are typically 85 degrees Fahrenheit (29 degrees Celsius). Ocean depth also impacts temperatures. The temperature at the ocean floor, the bottom of the ocean, is drastically colder than at the surface.

DID YOU KNOW

The seahorse is one of the only fish that swims in a vertical, or straight up and down, position!

Biodiversity and adaptations also radically change with ocean depth. Imagine you're traveling out into the ocean, farther and farther from shore, into deeper and darker waters. Eventually the floor drops down dramatically.

Scientists divide the ocean into zones, or levels, according to depth and the amount of sunlight each zone receives. When you splash in the waters at an ocean shore, you're in the **sunlight zone**.

DID YOU KNOW?

The world's largest creature, the endangered blue whale, inhabits the blue waters of the sunlight zone. This beautiful behemoth weighs a massive 150 tons (136 metric tons) and stretches to an astonishing 100 feet (30.5 meters) in length. If a blue whale could stand on its tail, it would be as tall as the Lincoln Memorial in Washington, D.C.!

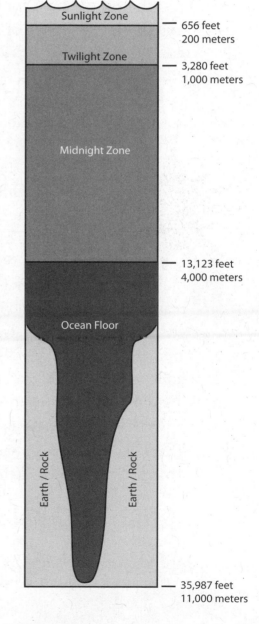

Sunlight Zone

656 feet
200 meters

Twilight Zone

3,280 feet
1,000 meters

Midnight Zone

13,123 feet
4,000 meters

Ocean Floor

Earth / Rock   Earth / Rock

35,987 feet
11,000 meters

Not surprisingly, this clear, light zone features the greatest biodiversity. You've learned that plants require sunlight to perform photosynthesis. Here in the sunlight zone, seagrasses and algae thrive.

Close to 90 percent of the ocean's living things inhabit the sunlight zone. That's why brightly colored coral reefs, which are teeming with life, are called "rainforests of the sea." Here, you'll find seals, sea turtles, sharks, lobsters, crabs, and brilliantly colored fish.

Words to Know

sodium chloride: salt, a clear compound found in nature, used to season food.

sunlight zone: the ocean zone that sunlight penetrates, where photosynthesis can occur and plants can grow.

Try This

Which is heavier, freshwater or salt water? Find out! You'll need a measuring cup, water, a jar, a scale, and table salt. First, fill the measuring cup with one cup of tap water. Then weigh it. Now, pour this freshwater into the jar. Add about one-eighth cup more tap water. Stir in salt. Gradually add as much as you can dissolve in the jar without making the water overflow. Now, pour one cup of the salt water into the measuring cup. Weigh it. You should discover that the salt water weighs more. That's because it's **denser**—it has more **mass** than freshwater in the same amount of space.

Rainforests of the Sea

You've learned that symbiosis is a win-win partnership between plants and animals of differing species. Colorful coral reefs are amazing examples of symbiosis. They are a combination of living animals and the skeletons of dead ones.

JUST FOR LAUGHS

Q: Why did the barracuda swim across the coral reef?
A: To get to the other tide!

Have you ever found a chunk of coral washed up on a beach? It looks like a lump of rock with lots of holes. Coral is actually a kind of limestone. That's rock formed from the shells and skeletons of marine animals. How do immense coral reefs form? These incredible water rainforests start with a microscopic, tentacled animal called a coral polyp. The polyp attaches itself to an underwater rock. Algae live within the cells of the coral, using the coral for protection and supplying it with food.

As the polyp reproduces, it creates a colony. That's a group of polyps attached together. To create their own skeletons, polyps use

DID YOU KNOW

With its crinkles and creases, brain coral looks like a human brain!

Words to Know

denser: more mass in the same space.

mass: the amount of physical matter in an object.

calcium carbonate: a compound found in animal bones that forms limestone.

twilight zone: the ocean zone reached by some sunlight, but not enough to allow photosynthesis to occur.

word exploration

An *aquanaut* is an underwater explorer. The Latin prefix *aqua* means "water." The Greek suffix *naut* comes from the word *nautical. Naut* means "explorer or voyager." What other words do you know that contain aqua? How about naut?

DID YOU KNOW

Pearls are the only gems found in living creatures, protected in mollusks such as oysters. Like coral reefs, pearls are formed from calcium carbonate.

calcium from sea water. They produce **calcium carbonate**, or limestone, over their lower bodies. In time, the living polyps die—and add to the coral reef. How? Their limestone skeletons become part of the reef. The skeletons are like building blocks that add onto the reef as living polyps clamp on them and grow. It's a slow process though—it takes nearly 10,000 years for a coral reef to form!

Deeper, Darker Zones

As you descend into the deeper waters of the **twilight zone**, you'll notice that light is limited. It's a good thing deep-sea creatures are adapted with stellar eyesight!

Earth's Explorers

In 1979, quanaut Sylvia Earle took the plunge to the lowest ocean depths ever explored! A marine botanist and NOAA's former Chief Scientist, Earle dove off the coast of Oahu at the age of 44. Wearing a pressurized diving suit, called a Jim, Earle submerged to 1,250 feet below the surface of the ocean to explore the inky Twilight Zone.

Consider the hatchet fish, with a scrunched body that resembles a small axe. Its bulging, tube-shaped eyes point up so it can spot food drifting overhead. The bizarre-looking barreleye fish boasts a see-through head. Its tubular eyes roll upward. The wary fish is able to see predators through its transparent head and zip to safety. Then its eyes rotate forward when the barrelhead chomps on prey.

By the time you plunge into the **midnight zone**, it's pitch black. How do sea creatures live in total darkness? With extreme adaptations!

Some deep-sea creatures survive by providing their own light in murky waters. **Bioluminescence** is an adaptation that allows both Twilight and Midnight Zoners, such as squid, flashlight fish, and anglerfish, to glow in the dark, using special chemicals present in their bodies. Consider the vampire squid, so named because it has webbing that flutters out from behind it like Dracula's cape. **Photophores**, organs that produce light, cover the vampire squid's body. It can turn on its lights to attract both mates and prey, as well as startle and temporarily blind predators.

DID YOU KNOW

The deep-sea shrimp actually vomits glowing goop to defend itself from attackers and make a quick getaway!

DID YOU KNOW

Plastic is forever. It never **biodegrades**. Scientists studying an albatross that died after consuming garbage discovered a bit of plastic in its stomach that contained a serial number. That number came from a World War II plane that was gunned down over the Pacific Ocean in 1944.

Threats to the Marine Biome

Climate change threatens the earth's oceans as much as it threatens the terrestrial biomes. Increased water temperatures affect ecosystems. One example is the danger faced by coral reefs. Warmer waters stress sensitive coral. When stressed, coral tosses out algae, which provides coral's dazzling colors as well as food for survival. The coral starves to death. Drained of vibrant color, it looks bleached.

Carbon dioxide dissolved in ocean water not only weakens the skeletons of corals so that they are more easily damaged, it also interferes with the formation of shells in shellfish.

The Ocean Floor

The underwater landscape is amazing, filled with soaring mountains and vast canyons! The ocean has many submerged volcanoes that are very active, and violently so. Take the Pacific Ocean's Ring of Fire. This boomerang-shaped stretch of volcanic activity reaches from the waters off New Zealand and around the Philippines. It swings up to Alaska and down to the coasts of North and South America. The Ring of Fire hosts about 75 percent of the earth's volcanoes, both dormant and active. Underwater eruptions and earthquakes rock the waves.

Another huge threat drifts aimlessly in the Pacific Ocean between California and Hawaii. An immense island of floating garbage—double the size of Texas—may contain more than 3.5 million tons (3.2 million metric tons) of tattered plastic bags, bobbing pellets, smashed toys, and bits of plastic bottles.

This "trash stew," mostly made of plastic, threatens animal life. Dolphins, albatrosses, and other seabirds become entangled in bags or mistakenly gobble down plastic pellets. Toxins in the plastics poison animal life, or the trash causes severe injuries and even death through choking or clogged intestines.

In the vast, interconnected web of life, people are impacted by trash and pollutants in the oceans, too. Fish eat the plant life that floats in the toxic waters. Then we eat the fish that have consumed the **toxins**. In addition, trash contaminates our precious beaches. What can you do? Cut down on your use of plastic products, and always recycle any plastic you can.

Words to Know

midnight zone: the ocean zone where there is no sunlight.

bioluminescence: a chemical reaction that allows deep-sea creatures to produce their own light.

photophores: special organs in the bodies of deep-sea creatures that allow them to produce light.

biodegrade: to decay or break down naturally.

toxin: poison or harmful substance.

Make a
BLUBBER MITT

For animals that live in the marine biome overlapping the tundra biome, such as walruses, polar bears, harp seals, sea lions, and penguins, blubber is important for survival. Blubber not only keeps these animals warm, but also provides them with **buoyancy**, or the ability to float. Make a blubber mitt to discover how this remarkable fat works to insulate animals and protect them from freezing temperatures. Is there snow on the ground where you live? Just for fun, you can substitute a tub of snow for the ice water in this experiment!

1 Cover your workspace with the drop cloth or plastic sheet. Slip on one plastic glove. Then spread about one tablespoon of lard or vegetable shortening on top of the glove—across the back of the hand and inside the palm.

2 Pull the second glove over the lard-covered glove. To prevent lard from oozing out and water from seeping in later, fold the cuff of the bottom glove over the top glove.

3 With your free hand, position the lard so it's evenly spread over your gloved hand.

Supplies

- drop cloth or plastic sheet
- large tub of water with ice cubes
- lard or solid vegetable shortening
- two right-handed or two left-handed recyclable plastic gloves
- stopwatch (optional)

4 What do you predict will happen when you plunge both hands into the tub of ice water? Test it out! You should notice that the lard acts as an insulator. It protects your hand from experiencing the coldness of the water, while keeping your body heat from escaping.

5 Have a friend or family member use the stopwatch or simply count to determine how many seconds you keep each hand in the water. How do the times compare? Did you feel any cold through the blubber mitt? What conclusions can you draw about blubber?

Words to Know

buoyancy: the ability to float.

Chapter 11

What Goes AROUND Comes Around

Whew! You've finished your journey around the world and are right back where you started, in your own backyard.

Use your knowledge of biomes to consider your role in the web of life. Some biomes seem remote, as if you couldn't possibly have an impact on them. But in the interconnected global environment, what goes around comes around. You can be like a domino that starts a ripple effect of positive influences on the planet!

In the last 100 years, the earth's temperature has risen by 1 degree Fahrenheit. Sounds pretty puny, doesn't it? As we've seen, though, the impact of global warming is enormous. It affects the entire planet, melting its ice caps and raising sea levels, parching its savannas and increasing the spread of deserts. Think about what you can do to benefit the environment. What actions can you take? How can you inspire others to do the same?

Walk, Pedal, and Roll

Start off by reducing your **carbon footprint**. That's the impact your activities have on the environment when they produce carbon dioxide. Walk, pedal your bike, or roll on your skateboard whenever possible. It's good for your body, as well as the environment. When traveling longer distances, take the bus or help your family organize a carpool.

Plastic Water Bottles

How many cast-off plastic bottles have you spotted around your stomping grounds lately? They're everywhere! In a single year, manufacturers use 1.5 million tons (1.3 million metric tons) of plastic to produce them. Too many people drink bottled water away from home, at places such as sporting events, amusement parks, and concerts. When crowds clear out, they leave mounds of these discarded containers behind.

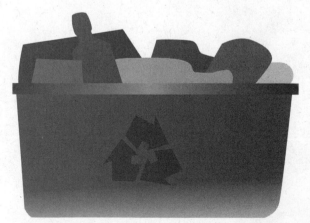

Words to Know

carbon footprint: the direct effect an individual's actions and lifestyle have on the environment in terms of carbon dioxide emissions, which contribute to global warming.

Energy Vampires

These dastardly villains suck energy in your home 24/7. How? They endlessly guzzle electricity. Did you know that even when you switch off computers, DVD players, and other electronics, they still consume energy if they're plugged in? You cell phone charger uses electricity even when your phone isn't charging. Here's a quick fix. Ask an adult to plug all the electronics into a single power strip. Then flick off the strip when you've finished watching TV or using the computer.

Try to avoid buying bottled water whenever you can. Instead, carry water with you in a reusable, eco-friendly container. While you're at it, don't stop with water bottles. Ask your family to swap juice boxes for larger cans or bottles, and divvy the jumbo containers into smaller, reusable ones. And grab the bulk size instead of buying 12 single-serving bags of chips. That way, you'll cut down on the packaging materials you throw away. And don't forget to reuse or recycle paper, plastics, cans, and other materials you do use.

Does It *Have* to Be New?

When you slip into your favorite old pair of jeans, you know that new doesn't necessarily mean better! Before you buy something new, find out if you can borrow or swap for the item. Or purchase a gently used one at a yard sale or thrift shop. Better yet, bring your creativity into play and discover a way to reuse something you already own in a whole new way so you don't need new at all!

Here are 10 actions you can dive into right away to make a difference on Earth.

Ten Tweaks You Can Make

●   Take showers instead of baths to conserve water. Tubs require 70 gallons (265 liters) of water to fill, while showers use 25 gallons on average (95 liters).

●   The amount of water you use in your shower depends, of course, on how long you spend there. So while you're at it, shorten your shower by one minute, or more than that if you take long showers. (Hey, you'll gain extra time to sleep!)

●   Dentists recommend you brush your pearly whites for two full minutes, two times a day. It's not a good idea to chisel time off there. But, as you brush your choppers, switch off the faucet. Why? If you run the water for that two minutes, you waste two gallons of water.

●   Drip, drip, drip! Leaky faucet? Tightly turn it off. Don't let a valuable resource dribble down the drain.

●   Collect rainwater, and use it to water houseplants, your desertarium, or your hummingbird garden.

●   Don't dawdle as you select a snack from the fridge. Grab the snack and close the door as quickly as you can to save energy.

●   Switch off the lights when you leave a room.

●   Turn off all electronics when you're finished using them.

●   When you enter and leave your house, shut the door quickly. The furnace or air conditioner will require less energy to do its job.

●   Paper or plastic? Neither! Tote a reusable bag when you go shopping.

What Else Can You Do?

Here are seven more things your family can do to help the environment and stop global warming. You can help save the planet and the biomes on it.

- **Plant a tree.** Trees take carbon dioxide out of the atmosphere and put oxygen into the atmosphere. A tree is like you own air-purifying machine.

- **Switch to compact florescent lightbulbs.** Not only do they use less electricity, they last much longer. Your parents will thank you for saving them money!

- **Keep your tires properly inflated.** You'll use less fuel and produce less carbon dioxide—and save money too.

- **Buy local products when you can.** Not only will you support your local farmer or store, you'll save all that fuel required to ship that product from across the country.

- **Eat less meat.** You don't have to give it up, but eating meat one less day per week can make a difference. Animals and the production of meat are huge producers of greenhouse gases.

- **Vote with your wallet.** Buy products with minimal packaging when possible and generate less trash. When you buy organic, you choose products grown without chemical fertizers. These chemicals pollute the water and use energy to produce. Next time your family needs a new appliance, choose one that's energy efficient.

- **Do a carbon footprint audit for your family.** Check out carbonfootprint.com or one of the other online sites. When you see how your individual actions contribute to your carbon footprint you can take steps to change your behavior—and reduce your footprint.

Take a Walkabout to
EXPLORE YOUR HOME TURF

You've traveled the globe and explored its biomes. Now it's time to dig out that recycled paper you created way back at the beginning of the book. Then wander into the great outdoors and take in the sights with a fresh set of eyes.

1 Zero in on a target ecosystem to explore. It might be a fallen log, a cactus, or a sunny patch in a grassy field.

2 With the binoculars, study the area. Then use the magnifying glass to take a closer look. What living things do you notice? How about nonliving things? Do the plants and animals that you see seem to demonstrate any special adaptations to their environment? Do any of them have camouflage? What about the subnivian life that naturalist Pam Otto described? How are today's weather conditions typical of the climate in which you live? What might threaten the environment? Record your observations and thoughts in your journal.

3 Use the thermometer to determine the temperature. Record it, and describe the weather conditions in your journal.

4 Slip on the gardening gloves, and turn over a patch of earth. You've investigated soil before. How does this sample compare? Jot your impressions in your journal.

Supplies

- binoculars
- magnifying glass
- journal and pencil
- thermometer
- garden gloves
- garden hand shovel
- scrap paper
- colored pencils
- decorated recycled paper

5 Return home, and use a sheet of scratch paper to compose a haiku about your target ecosystem. Haiku is a traditional form of Japanese poetry that describes and celebrates nature or the seasons. Haiku are not rhymed. They contain three lines with 17 syllables: five in the first line, seven in the second line, and five in the third line. Here's an example:

Leaves flutter like wings

Orange as autumn's pumpkins

They fall in crisp piles

When you're happy with your haiku, copy your it on your recycled paper and illustrate it. Share it with a friend or family member, and then hang it in a special place!

active layer: the layer of soil that melts in the summer.

adapt: changes a plant or animal makes to survive in new or different conditions.

adaptation: the development of physical or behavioral changes to survive in an environment.

aerate: to create channels that allow air to flow through.

air mass: body of air that spreads over a wide area.

altitude sickness: a medical condition that occurs in high altitudes. It is caused by low oxygen levels in the blood and tissues of the body. Its symptoms include fatigue, nausea, and dizziness.

altitude: height above sea level.

analyze: to study and examine.

annual: plants that flower and die in one season. New ones grow the next year from seeds.

aquatic: related to water.

archaeologist: someone who studies ancient cultures by looking at what they left behind.

arid: very dry, receiving little rain.

ascend: climb, move upward.

atmosphere: the mixture of gases that surround a planet.

atom: the smallest particle of all matter.

axis: an imaginary line down the middle of a sphere around which it rotates.

biodegrade: to decay or break down naturally.

biodiversity: the range of living things in an ecosystem.

bioluminescence: a chemical reaction that allows deep-sea creatures to produce their own light.

biome: a large natural area with a distinctive climate, geology, set of water resources, and group of plants and animals that are adapted for life there.

biosphere: the area of the earth and its atmosphere inhabited by living things.

blubber: an insulating layer of fat underneath an animal's skin, that helps keep the animal warm.

boom: a floating barrier used to contain oil spilled in water.

boreal forest: the coniferous forest biome.

buoyancy: the ability to float.

burrows: underground holes and tunnels where animals live.

buttresses: thick, aboveground roots that support tall trees.

calcium carbonate: a compound found in animal bones that forms limestone.

camouflage: the colors or patterns that allow a plant or animal to blend in with its environment.

canopy: an umbrella of trees over the forest.

carbon dioxide: an odorless, colorless gas formed from the burning of fossil fuels like gas and the decomposition of organic substances such as dead plants and animals. Carbon dioxide is a greenhouse gas that contributes to climate change and global warming.

carbon footprint: the direct effect an individual's actions and lifestyle have on the environment in terms of carbon dioxide emissions, which contribute to global warming.

carnivore: an animal that eats only other animals.

carrion: the dead and rotting body of an animal.

centripetal forces: forces that pull a moving object toward a center area.

chlorophyll: a pigment that makes plants green, used in photosynthesis to capture light energy.

circumference: the distance around a circle.

circumnavigate: to travel completely around something.

clearcut logging: a process in which all or almost all the trees in an area are chopped down.

climate: average weather patterns in an area over a period of many years.

coarse: composed of large particles.

competition: the struggle between living things for food, water, sunlight, and other resources.

coniferous trees: cone-bearing trees, often with needles for leaves. These trees do not lose their leaves each year.

crude oil: liquid petroleum that is extracted from the ground, but not yet transformed into gasoline, engine oil, diesel oil, kerosene, and other petroleum-based products.

currents: constantly moving masses of water.

data: information from tests or experiments.

deciduous trees: trees that shed their leaves each year.

decomposers: bacteria, fungi, and worms that break down wastes and dead plants and animals.

deforestation: the process through which forests are cleared to use land for other purposes.

degree: unit of measure of latitude. One degree of latitude equals 1/360 of a circle. The North Pole is 90 degrees north latitude, while the South Pole is 90 degrees south latitude.

denser: more mass in the same space.

desertification: the transformation of non-desert into desert, usually due to lack of water, deforestation, and/or overgrazing.

dormant: when plants are not actively growing during the winter.

drought: long, dry spell without rain.

dung: solid animal waste.

ecoregion: a large area, smaller than a biome, that has its own climate, geology, plants, and animals.

ecosystem: an interdependent community of living and nonliving things and their environment.

element: a basic substance, such as gold or oxygen, made of only one kind of atom.

elevation: height above sea level.

environment: everything in nature, living and nonliving, including plants, animals, soil, rocks, and water.

equator: the imaginary line around the planet halfway between the North and South Poles.

erosion: the gradual wearing away of rock or soil by water and wind.

Eurasia: the land mass of Europe and Asia.

evergreen: a tree that keeps its leaves or needles throughout the year.

extinction: the death of an entire species so that it no longer exists.

fault: a crack in the earth's surface that can cause earthquakes.

fauna: the animal life in an ecosystem.

fertile: rich in nutrients and good for growing plants.

fire-resistant: something that doesn't burn.

flora: the plant life in an ecosystem.

food chain: a series of plants and animals connected by their feeding relationships, with each new link in the food chain depending on the link below as a source of food.

food web: interrelated food chains.

forage: to wander from place to place in search of food.

frostbite: a medical condition in which skin and other tissues of the body are damaged by being frozen or partially frozen.

gaping: an adaptation in which a crocodile opens its mouth to regulate heat.

geological events: earthquakes, volcanic eruptions, and erosion.

geology: the rocks, minerals, and physical structure of an area.

germinate: to begin to grow from a seed.

glacier: an enormous mass of frozen snow and ice that moves across the earth's surface.

greenhouse effect: when gases such as carbon dioxide, methane, and water vapor permit sunlight to pass through but also trap solar radiation, causing the warming of the earth's surface.

greenhouse gas: a gas that traps heat in the earth's atmosphere and contributes to the greenhouse effect and global warming.

habitat: a plant or animal's home, which supplies it with food, water, and shelter.

herbivore: an animal that eats only plants.

hibernate: to sleep through the winter.

hull: a ship's body.

humus: decaying organic matter made from dead plant and animal material.

hypothermia: a dangerous condition caused by exposure to cold where body temperatures plunge to levels that are life-threatening.

invasive species: a non-native plant or animal species that enters a new ecosystem and harms it.

Krummholz Line: the highest elevation where krummholz trees grow.

krummholz: stunted trees growing just above the treeline on a mountain.

larvae: the worm-shaped form of a young insect (like a caterpillar) before it becomes an adult.

latitude: imaginary lines around the earth parallel to the equator.

liana: a woody vine that wraps itself around the trunks and branches of trees in an effort to reach the sunlight.

lichen: a patchy plant that is a combination of fungi and algae.

marsupial: a mammal that has a pouch where its young develop.

mass: the amount of physical matter in an object.

meteorologist: someone who studies the earth's atmosphere and forecasts the weather.

midnight zone: the ocean zone where there is no sunlight.

migrate: to move from one environment to another when seasons change.

nocturnal: describes an animal that is active at night instead of during the day.

Northern Hemisphere: the half of the planet north of the equator.

nutrients: substances that organisms need to live and grow.

omnivore: an animal that eats both plants and animals.

organic: of living things, or developing naturally.

organic matter: decaying plants and animals.

GLOSSARY

organism: something living, such as a plant or animal.

overgraze: when animals eat plants at a rate faster than the plants can grow back or be replaced by new plants.

overhunting: when an animal is hunted in great numbers, so much that their population falls to low levels. This can cause extinction.

pampas: term for temperate grassland in South America, especially Argentina.

peat: waterlogged, decomposed organic matter.

pelt: animal skin.

perennials: plants that flower and live for more than one season.

permafrost: permanently frozen subsoil and rock just beneath the surface of the ground.

photophores: special organs in the bodies of deep-sea creatures that allow them to produce light.

photosynthesis: the process through which plants create food, using light as a source of energy.

plains: term for temperate grassland, primarily used in the United States, but also in Canada.

plates: sheets of drifting solid rock on the earth's surface.

poaching: illegal hunting or fishing.

pollinating: transferring pollen from the male parts of the plant to the female parts.

porous: full of many little holes so water passes through.

prairie: term for temperate grassland, primarily used in Canada, but also in the United States.

predator: an animal that hunts another animal for food.

prehensile: able to grasp things.

prevailing wind: the most common wind in an area.

prey: animals hunted by other animals.

pulmonary edema: a medical condition in which the lungs fill with fluids and swell, making breathing difficult.

regolith: layer of loose rock, also called weathered bedrock.

rotation: turning around a fixed point.

savanna: term for tropical grassland.

social: describes animals that prefer to live in groups, rather than by themselves.

sodium chloride: salt, a clear compound found in nature, used to season food.

solid bedrock: layer of solid, unweathered rock.

sorghum: an important cereal crop grown in tropical areas, often used to feed livestock.

species: a type of animal or plant.

sprouts: shoots that grow from plants.

steppe: term for temperate grassland in Russia and the Ukraine.

strata: layers of the forest.

subnivian: the ground area below a layer of snow and above soil.

subsoil: layer beneath topsoil.

sunlight zone: the ocean zone that sunlight penetrates, where photosynthesis can occur and plants can grow.

symbiosis: a relationship between two different species of organisms in which each gains benefits from the other.

taiga: another name for the coniferous forest biome.

temperate: not extreme in terms of climate or weather.

terrestrial: related to land.

The Ice: the nickname for Antarctica.

timberline: also called the treeline—the elevation or limit beyond which trees do not grow in mountains or northern latitudes.

topsoil: the top layer of soil.

torrential: flowing intensely in large quantities.

toxin: poison or harmful substance.

transpiration: the evaporation of water from plants, usually through tiny pores in their leaves called stomata.

Tropic of Cancer: a line of latitude north of the equator, marking the northernmost point at which the sun can appear directly overhead at noon.

Tropic of Capricorn: a line of latitude south of the equator, marking the southernmost point at which the sun can appear directly overhead at noon.

tsunami: an abnormally large, destructive wave caused by an underwater earthquake.

twilight zone: the ocean zone reached by some sunlight, but not enough to allow photosynthesis to occur.

understory: the second layer of the forest, made up of saplings.

ungulates: mammals with hooves.

veldt: term for temperate grassland in South Africa.

visibility: the distance someone can see during certain weather conditions.

vortex: a rapidly whirling spiral of air or water.

RESOURCES

Books to Explore

Cherry, Lynn. *What We Know About Our Changing Climate: Scientists and Kids Explore Global Warming.* Dawn Publications, 2008.

Davis, Barbara J. *Biomes and Ecosystems.* Gareth Stevens, 2007.

Olien, Rebecca. *Kids Care! 60 Ways to Make a Difference for People, Animals, and the Environment.* Ideal Publications, 2007.

Parker, Steve. *100 Things You Should Know About Endangered Animals.* Barnes & Noble, 2008.

Reilly, Kathleen M. *Planet Earth: 25 Environmental Projects You Can Build Yourself.* Nomad Press, 2008.

Rothschild, David. *Earth Matters: An Encyclopedia of Ecology.* DK Publishing, 2008.

Simon, Seymour. *Earth: Our Planet in Space.* Simon and Schuster, 2003.

Thornhill, Jan. *This Is My Planet: The Kids' Guide to Global Warming.* Maple Tree Press, 2007.

VanCleave, Janice. *Science Around the World: Activities on Biomes From Pole to Pole.* John Wiley & Sons, 2004.

Weigel, Marlene. *Encyclopedia of Biomes.* U-X-L, 2000.

Wexo, John B. *Endangered Animals (Zoobooks Series.)* Wildlife Education, 2001.

Wines, Jacquie. *You Can Save the Planet: 50 Ways You Can Make a Difference.* Scholastic, 2008.

Biomes Websites

Center for Educational Technology, Biomes Module
http://www.cotf.edu/ete/modules/
msese/earthsysflr/biomes.html

Enchanted Learning, Biomes
http://www.enchantedlearning.com/biomes/

NASA's Earth Observatory
http://earthobservatory.nasa.
gov/Laboratory/Biome/

University of California Museum of
Paleontology's Biome Exhibit
http://www.ucmp.berkeley.edu/
exhibits/biomes/index.php

World Wildlife Federation's Main
Biomes of the World
http://www.panda.org/news_facts/education/
webfieldtrips/major_biomes/index.cfm

Cool Websites for Kids

Calculate your household's carbon footprint
http://www.nature.org/initiatives/
climatechange/calculator/

EPA Environmental Kids Club
http://www.epa.gov/kids/

EEK! Environmental Education for Kids
http://www.dnr.state.wi.us/eek/

Inch in a Pinch: Saving the Earth
http://inchinapinch.com/

Kids Do Ecology
http://www.nceas.ucsb.edu/nceas-web/kids/

National Geographic Kids
http://kids.nationalgeographic.com/

NOAA for Kids
http://oceanservice.noaa.gov/kids

USDA Forest Service
http://www.na.fs.fed.us/spfo/ce/
content/for_kids/index.cfm

 # INDEX